Shopping Your Way Across

KENTUCKY

Shopping Your Way Across

KENTUCKY

101 MUST PLACES TO SHOP

GARY P. WEST

Acclaim Press ™

MORLEY, MISSOURI

Acclaim Press
— Your Next Great Book —

P.O. Box 238
Morley, MO 63767
(573) 472-9800
www.acclaimpress.com

Cover Design: M. Frene Melton

Book Design by:

GRAPHIC DESIGN

Designer: Mary Ellen Sikes

Library of Congress Cataloging-in-Publication Data

West, Gary P.
  Shopping your way across Kentucky : 101 must places to shop / by Gary P. West.
      p. cm.
  Includes index.
  ISBN-13: 978-1-935001-11-9 (alk. paper)
  ISBN-10: 1-935001-11-6 (alk. paper)
  1. Shopping--Kentucky--Guidebooks. 2. Stores, Retail--Kentucky--Guidebooks.
  3. Specialty stores--Kentucky--Guidebooks. 4. Kentucky--Guidebooks. I. Title.

  TX336.5.K4W47 2008
  381'.1109769--dc22

                                        2008033687

Printed in the United States of America
First Printing: 2008
10 9 8 7 6 5 4 3 2 1

Additional copies may be purchased from Acclaim Press.

Contents

Dedication

This book is dedicated to my mother, Charleene West, and her two sisters, Mary Laura McCay and Dorothy Malone. All three shopped early and often and bought things whether they needed them or not.

Growing up in the small Warren County town of Smiths Grove, the three "Jones girls" learned the art of buying and selling at an early age from their father Charlie Jones, a farmer by trade.

More often than not, the process of the purchase was the prize, not the necessity of the item.

"It was such a good buy I couldn't pass it up," was the overriding theme. "It might come in handy someday."

Pictured from left: Charleene West, Dorothy Malone (standing on ground), and Mary Laura McCay.

Preface

A book on shopping could easily be written about shops only in Louisville or Lexington, or you might include shops from Bowling Green, Covington, Owensboro and Paducah. They all have wonderful shopping from a "bigger city" standpoint.

However, this book was written to reflect the incredible shopping opportunities that exist in smallest of Kentucky towns, as well as the larger ones.

These are special unique stores literally in your back yard.

Kentuckians don't have to travel hundreds of miles to shop, although it is fun to do on occasion. Readers are encouraged to look around and see what's at hand.

The absence of a certain shop, store, or business, doesn't mean they are not deserving. It only means that there was not enough room in these pages to include everyone.

As you browse through these pages you might be surprised at how many stores are owned by several stubborn generations who have refused to give up. For the most part they have been reluctant to place quantity over quality.

Introduction

Shopping Your Way Across Kentucky…101 Must Places to Shop does not mean that stores and shops not listed in these pages are not worthy, because there are literally hundreds of good places to shop in Kentucky.

What you find here are 101 unique shops, stores and districts. Many of these stores were recommended by people in the tourism and hospitality business. These are places they often tell visitors about, and in some cases even consider a tourist attraction. Other stores were pointed out as being unique, and in some cases one-of-a-kind.

Shopping, like eating, can be fun, and shopping, like eating, to some, is a necessity.

I want to say almost everything I know about shopping, I owe to my mom. She was a wheeler dealer. I remember as a little boy going with her to buy a refrigerator. She made the salesman earn his money that day. She would not accept someone pointing in the direction of refrigerators and saying, "They're over there." No sir, in order for my mom to be sold, that salesman had to pound on the side of the appliance to prove to her it would not dent. He then had to almost do a chin-up on the top shelf to show her it would support the milk, a big pitcher of Kool Aid, and giant jar of dill pickles. Back then there weren't any automatic ice makers, but it was important to my mom how many ice trays the freezer would hold.

And then there was the time she took me with her to look for a new record player. That's what they were called. But my mom had her sights set on something new. A hi-fi, short for high fidelity. It was the marketing buzz word and we were going to have one at our house. As expected, the salesman had to know what he was talking about. Nope, no "the hi-fis are over there," with this customer. Thank goodness the store had a supply of 45 rpm records, because my mom wanted to hear the sound from different distances from the hi-fi she liked. I would stand in one corner of the store and she would stand in another, all the while asking me if I could still hear it. "Of course I can," I told her.

She finally settled on a Magnavox, French provincial style cabinet model. It was like a piece of furniture, with built-in speakers, and two sliding tops that opened to a turntable, storage, and a nifty little knob that allowed you to switch from phono to radio, AM only.

We had been in the store well over an hour and it was late afternoon. There was still work to be done, however. Getting to an agreeable price between my mom and the salesman (who by now I had learned was also the owner of the store) was finally reached in about 15 minutes.

But my mom was still not through. Her final piece of the chase, and the deal, was when she said, "I'll take it if you can deliver it this afternoon."

Needless to say we didn't watch TV that night, but we did listen to some good music on our new hi-fi. Little did it matter that the cabinet style and color did not match anything else in the room. The important thing was we had a hi-fi.

Shopping is not restricted just to the female gender. For decades, if not centuries, women have unjustly been labeled as the big spenders when it comes to shopping.

Keep in mind shopping falls into two categories. First there's the essentials for life: food, clothing and shelter. And then there's shopping for what might be considered non-essential. That is things we could probably do without, but don't really want to.

That's where this book fits in. Inside these pages are varied assortments of things to buy, among them food, clothing, and yes, even shelter. But most, however, might be considered frivolous. Frivolous that is until you see that one certain item you cannot live without. At that point frivolous flies out the window.

I spent over twelve years working in the tourism/hospitality business. My objective was to bring people to Bowling Green. These people came individually, in small clusters, or in large groups. Either way there are two common denominators with each. They want to make sure there are plenty of places to eat and shop. The traveling public likes to do both, and plenty of it.

This leads me back to the part where women take what I think is a bum rap on shopping issues. How many times have you been shopping, perhaps at an outlet mall or historic district, and seen someone taking advantage of sidewalk benches outside the shops? My unofficial observation revealed it used to be only men who sat on these benches, but as of late I'm seeing more and more women.

Why?

Perhaps it's all about the signal.

Years ago my mom and dad "ran around" with a couple of their friends, often heading out on weekends to eat at an out-of-the-way restaurant and to bargain hunt.

When it came to the shopping part their friends had a signal, as they referred to it.

Whenever they found something they both really liked, one would say to the other, within ear-shot of the shopkeeper, "I'm not wild about it, do what you want, I'm going outside." That was the signal to buy it. And that's when one or the other would begin to bargain with the sales person.

"I don't know, he doesn't really want me to buy it," the conversation would go. In the meantime her husband would often be outside on one of those benches. And often they would get what they perceived to be a bargain on something they both wanted. The signal worked for them.

I'm not advocating this approach, but only relaying a shopping story I've told many times over the years.

So the next time you see a person sitting on one of those sidewalk benches, it could be they have given the signal and are only waiting for their bargain.

It's all about the signal.

To some, shopping is an inherent right. I've always thought so, as long as I had the money to indulge. I've always heard that the two things travelers like to do when they go someplace is to eat and shop, and not always in that order.

This book is all about shopping in Kentucky. There are 101 places to spend money. Some of these are more unusual than others, but nevertheless, they are in this book because in their own sort of way they are special.

Some are large and offer an array of merchandise, while others might feature only one item. Some are on the beaten path, some off.

Shopping Your Way Across Kentucky conjures up a broad range of stores, shops, and even a few places that serve food. The purpose of this book is to fulfill a desire that many of us have: to buy stuff.

Listed in these pages are businesses that offer a first class shopping experience. One of the criteria for inclusion was that the locals, when asked, would tell you to "not leave here without stopping in such and such place." It was usually that such and such place that made the book. The great thing about this book is the ripple effect it creates. If you go to a certain area because of one of the featured stores, there's a good possibility you will find several more shopping opportunities in the same area, if not right down the street. It could even be right next door.

Surprises abound in these pages. A big surprise! I mean some of these places are not what would immediately come to mind when thinking of places to shop. But some will become destination spots when it comes to unusual locations to spend money.

Shopkeepers across the state offer a wide assortment of wares. From the necessities of life, to frivolous and outlandish, shoppers can find it all in Kentucky.

Some Kentucky shops and stores offer for sale items from throughout the world. Others offer one-of-a-kind items, while a few will make just what you order, just for you.

There's nothing wrong with chain stores mind you, it's just that you won't find any of them in this book. The majority of the listed stores and shops are privately owned, with an occasional shop owned by the state. But even these offer up merchandise not readily found anywhere else.

Mom-and-pop type stores, many of which have been in business for decades, are the norm here. This is what makes Kentucky shopping so special.

The thought here is that shopping should be pleasant as well as entertaining. It should be combined with an enjoyable meal, and if traveling overnight, comfortable lodging. It's the total package that makes for a memorable experience.

Shopping in Kentucky is not just for the rich and famous, although some of them do live and shop here. Bargains galore can be found, but just remember that bargains are only as good as the quality of what you purchase. Some bargains are bargains after all.

Many times the true test of a store and what it sells is how long it has been in business. Those shops that have managed to "stay around" have done so because of the quality of what they sell, and customer service.

In spite of the box store discounters, these stores take pride in being competitive with much larger chain stores.

Shopping Your Way Across

KENTUCKY

ALLES BROTHERS FURNITURE COMPANY	HENDERSON, KY
BAKERS RACK	OWENSBORO, KY
BROADBENT COUNTRY HAMS	CADIZ, KY
COFFEE AND... BOOKS ON MAIN	HOPKINSVILLE, KY
CREATURES OF HABIT	PADUCAH, KY
EXCURSIONS	OWENSBORO, KY
HANSON SHOPPING DISTRICT	HANSON, KY
HAZEL ANTIQUES	HAZEL, KY
HENSON'S BROOMS & COUNTRY STORE	SYMSONIA, KY
KENTUCKY STATE PARK GIFT SHOPS	STATEWIDE
MENTOR HOUSE GALLERY	PADUCAH, KY
PATTI'S 1880 SETTLEMENT	GRAND RIVERS, KY
QUILT MUSEUM	PADUCAH, KY
SIMON'S SHOES	HENDERSON, KY
THE GIFT HORSE	MADISONVILLE, KY
UNCLE LEE'S	GREENVILLE, KY
VINTAGE ROSE EMPORIUM	MURRAY, KY

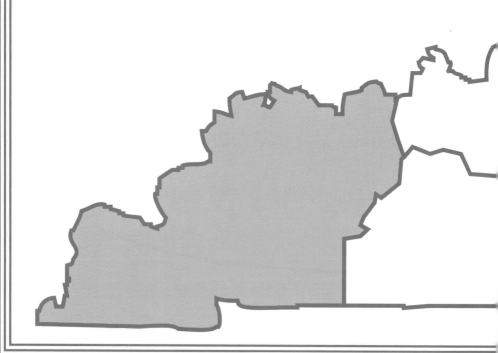

WESTERN REGION

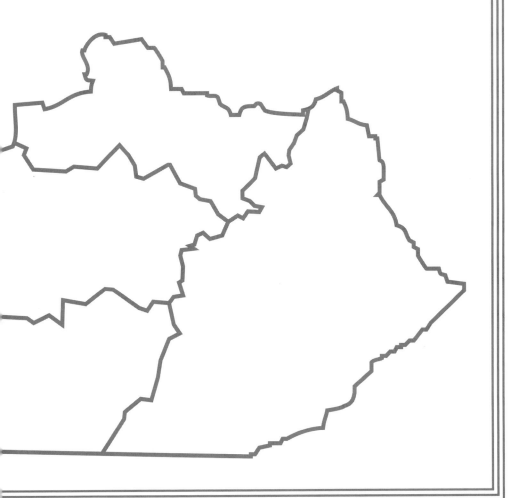

Alles Brothers Furniture Company
HENDERSON, KY

This is a furniture store that first opened in Henderson in 1899 and still prides itself in doing business the old fashion way, in that receipt and invoices are still handwritten.

Like most old successful businesses, Alles Furniture started small, but now occupies six buildings on First Street between Main and Elm. Although it takes pride in continuing old traditions, you can bet this full-line furniture store is up to snuff with the lines it sells.

John Sides has managed the store since 1982, but is quick to point out that it is the high standards established decades ago by owners Herman Alles and his sister Mary Frances, that have made this store what it is.

"I plan on continuing our low key approach to sales without pressure," says Sides. "And our no-pressure sales force will spend as much time as needed with customers to find the items they want."

Although the store might seem antiquated in some ways, Sides says it had the first large IBM computer for retailers in the area, as well as being the first store to offer a one year payment plan without interest.

The store even has a strong connection to furniture design that involves a popular piece still going strong today...the roll top desk. Jacob Alles, Herman's father, conceived the idea in his early 20s, and while his name is not on the patent, the credit nevertheless belongs to him. The company that Jacob and his brother John operated in 1871 had the name on the patent.

With all of the giant chain furniture stores operating today, places like Alles Brothers are truly a breath of fresh air. When you consider they survived World War I, the Great Depression, the flood of 1937, and World War II, when furniture making came to a halt because no stock was available, you are almost inclined to ask "how did they do it?"

SHOPPERS INFO

Address:
219 First Street
Hours:
7:30 a.m. – 5 p.m., Monday – Saturday
Closed Sunday
Phone:
270/827-3593
Area Attractions:
John J. Audubon State Park

Bakers Rack
OWENSBORO, KY

$\mathcal{S}$o often is the case it takes the closing of one store to create the opening of another.

This is the case of the Bakers Rack in Owensboro.

When Mary Dixon Baker started a small plant shop in 1974, she had no thoughts whatsoever that one day her store would become a wonderful shop of fine gifts and personal accessories. After the closing of Anderson's, a local downtown department store, suddenly there was a need for a place for customers to purchase china and bridal gifts. That was the beginning of the transformation of the little plant store into what you see today.

Shazam!

Nestled back in the corner of Wesleyan Park Plaza, on Frederica Street, the store offers a front entrance as well as one in the back. Most of the locals prefer the convenience of the back. Its attractive polka-dot awnings match the store's signature brown and white wrapping paper.

Upon entering, customers are immediately drawn to sparkling Waterford crystal, Arthur Court's pewter creations, highly popular Vera Bradley handbags, dozens of china patterns and a beautiful variety of high quality accents.

Displays are set up throughout the 10,000-square-foot store, much like you would see in a home, preferably your home.

"This gives shoppers inspiration for decorating their own homes," offers Anne Baker Leazenby, Mary Dixon's daughter.

One area may feature a beautifully polished antique dining table laden with crystal stemware and bone china just waiting for

a grand dinner party, while another vignette shows a fireplace setting, complete with fire screen, gleaming brass fire tools and a "sleeping" plush dog.

As fantastic as the inventory is and as attractive as the shop is, this, according to Anne, is not the heart of the business.

"Service is our specialty," she offers. "That's really how we've grown. We love working with new customers because we get to show them around the store. Our new customers often become our friends for a lifetime."

SHOPPERS INFO ?

Address:
2690 Frederica Street
Wesleyan Park Plaza
Hours:
10 a.m. – 6 p.m., Monday – Friday
10 a.m. – 5 p.m., Saturday
Closed Sunday
Phone:
270/684-6130
Area Attractions:
Bluegrass Music Museum, Festivals, Motorsports

19

Broadbent Country Hams
CADIZ, KY

For well over 80 years the Broadbent family has been making delicious country hams, and as the old saying goes, they must be doing something right.

Seven times this Trigg County ham store has had a ham that has been declared Grand Champion Ham at the Kentucky State Fair. For several years the winning ham has been auctioned for a charity cause, and the high bidder has paid well into the hundreds of thousands of dollars.

However, when you visit the Broadbent Store and Gift Shop in Cadiz, you can buy this mouth watering slow-cured ham for a whole lot less.

Broadbent's products, other than country ham, include bacon and sausage. The food items here are packaged for visitors to take with them.

Here are some of the items you can purchase at the store: uncooked country ham; family pack of ham, bacon, sausage, cheese and bread; boneless baked country ham with honey glaze; smoked country pork sausage; a package combo of country ham, bacon and sausage; breakfast combo; original hickory smoked country sliced bacon; hickory smoked sliced pepper bacon; and even a boneless smoked turkey breast.

Kentucky is known for country hams, and although there are many

businesses across the state that turn them out, Broadbent ranks among the top and has the pedigrees to prove it. With their special technique of blending honey, sugar and salt, and then slow-smoking their hams for six to twelve months, Broadbent has mastered a product that has become as much of a tradition in Kentucky as bourbon and horses.

With all this said, may I caution you not to overlook those incredible cheese spreads, some with bits of ham in it. Oh my!

SHOPPERS INFO

Address:
Hwy. 68/80 at I-24
5695 Hopkinsville Road
Hours:
8 a.m. – 6 p.m., Monday – Thursday
8 a.m. – 7 p.m., Friday & Saturday
9 a.m. – 6 p.m., Sunday
Phone:
270/522-6674
Area Attractions:
Lake Barkley State Resort Park

Tasty beverages, delicious food and a bountiful selection of great books. These two businesses, Coffee And... Books On Main, have combined under a single roof to give customers all the more reason to come into their stores, and when they do, to sit down and stay awhile.

Hilarie Dawson opened Coffee And... almost six years ago with a goal of serving up gourmet coffees, espresso drinks and teas. And with it came those plentiful lunch specials to include the freshly made chicken salad. Get there early and enjoy some made-fresh daily scones, muffins, brownies and cookies.

Of course, they have gift sets to include coffees, teas and mugs, but there's one in particular that you'll want to check out.

It's called a "flowering tea." The tea leaves have been sewn by hand and shaped into a pod. When hot water is poured over the pod it opens and a beautiful flower appears. It's a real treat for customers and makes for a unique gift.

Books On Main occupies the front area of the building, and books is their game. Lots and lots of them.

Best sellers, contemporary, Christian, fiction, children's and non-fiction are just some of the offerings.

Owners, Pam and Wayne Gulsby, are proud of their designated area recognizing Kentucky authors, and in particular three-time Pulitzer Prize winner Robert Penn Warren, a native of nearby Guthrie, Kentucky. There's also a large selection of books on world-renowned psychic Edgar Cayce. Cayce, a

Christian County native, is one of the more interesting characters to ever come out of Kentucky and you can find out all about him here.

The two businesses regularly sponsor a variety of events such as poetry readings, sing-alongs, and on Friday nights, live music.

This is a fun place to visit, relax, enjoy a snack, and find out if you have anything in common with Edgar Cayce.

SHOPPERS INFO ?

Address:
911 South Main Street
Hours:
8 a.m. - 5 p.m., Monday - Friday
9 a.m. - 2 p.m., Saturday
Phone:
270/881-5021
Area Attractions:
Trail of Tears Park

Creatures of Habit
PADUCAH, KY

It's a promise. You will not find another business like this in the book. Not even close.

Creatures of Habit costumes was opened in downtown Paducah in 1987, and owners, Natalya and Jack Cody, have created this extraordinary one-of-a-kind store, initially to outfit Paducah and the surrounding tri-state area with costumes. Not long after, they discovered people all over the country wanted their services.

With over 11,000 costumes, and half a million authentic period garments and accessories in stock for purchase or rental, it's no wonder it takes much of the four-story 1908 brick building to hold the inventory. The building itself is special. Blue and white, with a bright yellow awning and orange neon outlining the windows, make sure you know you're at the right place.

A few years ago, Creatures of Habit made a "Hollywood connection" and ever since, their services have been used in movies such as *In Country*, *Pink Cadillac*, *A League of Their Own*, and *Titanic*, just to mention a few.

This unique store carries make-up, wigs, beards, special effects, masks, and accessories to include footwear, costume jewelry, eyewear, gloves and canes.

Would you believe they also carry costumes from the Middle Ages, Colonial America, Victorian era, the 20th century and ethnic nations?

Mannequins of all ages and sizes, as well as props that include ship's wheels, coffins, palm trees, covered wagon, mummies, King's throne chairs, disco balls, and even a full-size bamboo rickshaw.

If you've got the imagination, this place has the "stuff" to pull it off.

Creatures of Habit supplies costumes to the professionals and the professional "wanna-bees." And get this, they even provide a service to help you develop a plot. Their expert resources can assist you in creating a visually dynamic production.

"The average cost of a costume rental is ranges from $25-$35," says Natalya. "And we carry adult and children sizes from a child size 6 to an adult XXXXL."

With a store like this, there is absolutely no excuse for not going to the big doings because you have nothing to wear. Walk on the wild side a bit.

SHOPPERS INFO

Address:
406 Broadway
Hours:
10 a.m. – 7 p.m., Monday – Saturday
Closed Sunday and major holidays
Phone:
270/442-2923
Area Attractions:
Quilt Museum, Flood Wall Murals

Excursions
OWENSBORO, KY

This is an upscale place to shop for ladies for trendy seasonal clothing and accessories.

Opened in 1983, many in Owensboro consider it THE place to shop. "We serve customers from a tri-state area," offers owner Jaye Evans. "And I like to think that our seasoned sales people are so good with customers that it is like having their own personal stylist."

Without question Excursions has all of the "fancy-smantzy" brands. One shopper was overheard to say, "you'd have to go the New York City to find these selections."

Keeping up with the ever-changing fashion scene is no doubt part of the success of this beautiful store, and with names like BCBG, Trina Turk and Nanette Lepore you can see why.

"We have this area's largest selection of premiere denim from Citizens for Humanity, Seven for All Mankind, Juicy and Joe's," Evans added.

Address:
2690 Frederica Street
Wesleyan Park Plaza
Hours:
10 a.m. – 6 p.m., Monday – Saturday
Phone:
270/926-8388
Area Attractions:
Bluegrass Music Museum, Festivals, Motorsports

*N*ever underestimate the fact that one person can make a difference. Teresa Anthony is proof of that.

Hanson is a small, no make that very small, community in Hopkins County, only a few miles from Madisonville. Just a few years ago Hanson might have been a ghost town, except for the presence of a post office, town hall, and a building that houses the fire truck.

Teresa had grown up in Hanson, and although she had physically lived away for years, she had never really left mentally.

"I loved Hanson and its old buildings," she says. "And when it all came together and there was an opportunity to buy up some of the buildings, I did."

She started with a few, buying and rehabbing, and now she owns a dozen. And what she has done with all this is simply amazing.

"Some very brave shop owners joined me in turning things around downtown," she says enthusiastically. "There is something now literally for everyone."

It's easy to see what Teresa is talking about when she points out an antique mall, two antique and collectible shops, a woodcarvers shop, book store and several more gift and home décor shops.

A pizza shop and two other eateries make sure no one goes hungry when they visit Hanson.

One of the shops, the Picket Fence, is in a building that, only a few years ago, was just a brick shell.

"It had no roof, floor, interior

walls, and had trees growing in it," points out Teresa. "You see it now and it is absolutely beautiful with its custom painted wood floor and 14-foot ceiling."

Wanamaker Lee's, Maple Leaf Lane, Back Door Creations, Miss Willie's Emporium, Apple House Gallery and Stony Creek Crafts are "must-see" shops when you come to Hanson.

For sometime Hanson has had the distinction of being the smallest historic district in Kentucky. But this wonderful little town, with buildings dating back to 1879, has a heart as big as any in the state.

SHOPPERS INFO ?

Address:
Halfway between Henderson and Hopkinsville on the Pennyrile Parkway
Hours:
Generally open 10 a.m. – 5 p.m., Tuesday – Saturday and until 6 p.m., Friday & Saturday
A few shops are open Sunday
Phone:
270/821-4171
Area Attractions:
Ruby Laffoon Log Cabin, John J. Audubon State Park

WESTERN

Hazel Antiques
HAZEL, KY

azel is a small community off the beaten path on the southern edge of Calloway County near the Tennessee border.

It may be small, but when it comes to antiques it's big, very big. Believe me, it's well worth the time and effort if antiques are your thing. It's only eight miles from Murray.

Some twelve shops totaling 500 dealers make Hazel a place for deal-seeking beginners all the way up to high-end collectors.

In Hazel, there are three things that make antiquing enjoyable: the range of merchandise is good, prices are affordable, and the clerks are very friendly and helpful. You don't have to buy a thing to have fun.

In the early 1980s, downtown Hazel was pretty much just a shell. But for the vision of a retired bricklayer who was passing through town and stopped to buy a soft drink, all that began to change after he opened an antique store.

Over the years the community has earned a reputation of being an antique Mecca, drawing customers on a regular basis from a five state area.

The twelve shops are open seven days a week for the convenience of shoppers, browsers or anyone else who takes the time to drive in. The enormous concentration of antiques is not matched anywhere else in the region.

Miss Martha's Antiques has

been going and growing since the summer of 1983.

"We were here when not many others were," offered owner Martha Price. "We've been doing this for a long time and love it."

Other shops include Horse's Mouth Antiques, Blue Moon Antiques, Its So Real, The Corner Shop, The Cabin, Tooter's Antique Mall, Memory Lane Antique Mall, Heart of Hazel Mall, Angelique's Antiques and Interiors, and Charlie's Antique Mall.

Charlie's has an old vintage 1950s-style soda fountain with hand-dipped ice cream, banana splits, malts and shakes.

All of these shops are first class and each has its own specialties, from furniture to art to glass to china to lamps.

On the first Saturday of October, the town plays host to its annual Hazel Day. It typically draws over 8,000 visitors who enjoy not only the shopping, but a parade, cakewalks, flea markets, music and plenty of food.

WESTERN

SHOPPERS INFO ?

Address:
U.S. Hwy. 641 in Calloway County
Hours:
Seven days a week
Phone:
270/492-8145
Area Attractions:
Antiques, Murray State University, Kentucky Lake

Henson's Brooms & Country Store
SYMSONIA, KY

Richard Henson's grandfather used to pedal the brooms he made from Paducah and western Kentucky, throughout southern Illinois, southeast Missouri and west Tennessee. That was in the 1930s, and he sold those brooms for 25 cents a piece.

Today, almost 80 years later, the Henson's are still pedaling brooms, but now it's out of a unique "country store" setting in Symsonia, a small town in Graves County.

"My grandfather's last words to me before he died were, "if you learn how to make a broom you will always have a job," Henson said.

At the time Henson was a teacher and basketball coach. He thought that's what he would always do. But those words kept tugging at him, and with the urging of his father, who was also a broom maker, he finally gave in and put his inherited broom-making equipment to good use.

"I started making the same broom that my dad and grandfather always made," he says. "The date was October 23, 1988. When I started making my own brooms, I felt I had finally found myself and my niche in life."

Henson was not content to just make "a" broom. He let his imagination take over, and now he makes 14 different styles of brooms, ranging in price from $3.00 to $50.00. Soon he had brooms all over the country and several foreign countries. Then he was asked to make brooms for the hit television show, *Dr. Quinn, Medicine Woman.* They ordered 300.

Because of natural story-telling ability, Henson takes his broom-making on the road and is a popular speaker and humorist. He says it's all because of that 25 cent broom his grandfather used to sell.

He and his wife Barbara and their children have changed their horse barn into a country store that takes on the appearance of a broom-making museum, and although the equipment is not for sale there are plenty of brooms, baskets, Amish products, sorghum, molasses, honey, hand-churned butter, maple syrup, straw hats, handmade soaps, walking sticks and wreaths that are.

His son Richard has taken up the craft and is now the fourth generation of R.N. Henson's to make brooms.

Participating in various craft competitions over the years, Henson has won his share of awards over potters, chair makers and other artisans whose work most people consider more artistic than broom making. "The broom is the Rodney Dangerfield of tools," he chuckles.

SHOPPERS INFO ?

Address:
1060 State Rt. 348 East
Hours:
Tuesday - Sunday
To make sure to see Henson actually making a broom, call ahead.
Phone:
270/851-8510 - call before you go!
Area Attractions:
Lakes, Quilt Museum, Flood Wall Murals

Kentucky State Park Gift Shops
STATEWIDE

Over the years Kentucky's State Parks have been recognized among the best in the nation. Their scenic beauty and often remote locations have set them apart and make them desirable places to visit. Whether it's the view of a pristine lake or a mountain top retreat, Kentucky State Park Resorts offer a comfortable setting at a good value.

But now many of these same parks offer top-of-the-line shopping. Naturally these gift shops concentrate on Kentucky products, from books, clothes, pottery, jewelry, garden décor, crafts and food products.

Blue Licks Battlefield
Carlisle, KY

Located near Carlisle, this first class gift shop carries high end merchandise that is often one-of-a-kind items.

Kentucky artisans display handmade pottery, baskets and paintings, as well as specialty things like painted gourds, walking sticks, soaps and floral arrangements. It goes on and on.

Blue Licks schedules many special events throughout the year to highlight not only their gift shop but the park and its surroundings as well.

John James Audubon Gift Shop
Henderson, KY

No where else in the Kentucky State Park System will you find such a concentration of gifts and merchandise. From Audubon reproduction prints, that include songbirds, birds of prey, and the ivory-billed woodpecker, to books on birding, bird houses, feeders and garden art, this shop is a shopper's delight.

Also popular here are the children's educational books, field guides and biographical books that relate to John Audubon's life and works.

Other Kentucky State Park Gift Shops

Carter Cave — Olive Hill, Ky
Barren River Lake — Lucas, Ky
Kentucky Dam Village — Gilbertsville, Ky
Jenny Wiley — Prestonsburg, Ky
Cumberland Falls — Corbin, Ky
Kenlake — Hardin, Ky
Natural Bridge — Slade, Ky
Pennyrile Forest — Dawson Springs, Ky
My Old Kentucky Home — Bardstown, Ky
Constitution Square — Danville, Ky
Dr. Thomas Walker — Barbourville, Ky
Buckhorn Lake — Buckhorn, Ky
Dale Hollow Lake — Burkesville, Ky
General Butler — Carrollton, Ky
Greenbo Lake — Greenup, Ky
Lake Barkley — Cadiz, Ky
Lake Cumberland — Jamestown, Ky
Pine Mountain — Pineville, Ky
Rough River Dam — Falls of Rough, Ky
Fort Boonesborough — Richmond, Ky
Old Mulkey Meeting House — Tompkinsville, Ky

SHOPPERS INFO

Address:
23 locations scattered throughout the state. Specific locations can be found at www.parks.ky.gov

Hours:
Varries by location and season

Phone:
Refer to www.parks.ky.gov

Area Atractions:
Each has its own attractions

Mentor House Gallery
PADUCAH, KY

Paulette Mentor may be only 5-feet tall, but she has an 18-foot imagination in the form of a stainless steel giraffe reaching for leaves on a second-floor balcony.

This and more can be seen at Mentor House Gallery in the lower Town Arts District in downtown Paducah.

The big giraffe has become a local landmark and recently has been joined in the front lawn by a baby giraffe leaning to sip water off the ground. Metal artist George Bondorra is the creator of the unusual art and because of it, and all of the other distinctive visuals, the Gallery has been featured on television's *HGTV.*

The Mentor House Gallery is a happening place. While this fine arts gallery provides an elegant setting for the unique, contemporary art exhibited, Paulette's diverse collection of art glass, paintings, sculptures and unusual gifts from artists around the country provides enjoyment for all ages.

If there's any stuffiness here, it is quickly put aside upon seeing the participatory art in the bathroom and the unusual ways of painting the walls.

This imaginative, cleaver presentation most certainly has a way of breaking the ice.

Another element that makes this place special is the artists' studio that is connected to the gallery.

"People enjoy seeing where the artist works, what products are used, and how the process comes together," offers Paulette.

She adds that visitors come to see her gallery because others tell them, "If you only have time to visit one gallery you must go to the Mentor House Gallery."

Paulette moved to Paducah in 2004 from Bremerton, Washington. With her she brought a vivid artistic eye and the ability to make it work in a pleasing, fun way. She's proud of the fact that visitors enjoy the gallery décor just as much as the art she has for sale.

SHOPPERS INFO ?

Address:
332 N. 6th Street
Hours:
12 noon - 5 p.m., Wednesday – Sunday
2nd Saturday of every month open until 8 p.m.
Phone:
270/442-1635
Area Attractions:
Flood Wall Murals, Quilt Museum, Creatures of Habit

When you think of Patti's, the first thing is usually food. That may not change anytime soon, but what will change is that Patti's is also a destination place to shop.

Behind the restaurant is the "settlement," a group of small shops that over the years has created a wonderful place to stroll from shop to shop.

The Tullar family has created a destination restaurant that in turn has led to destination shopping. On the grounds are six shops, each with a different theme. Located in reconstructed historic log cabins, original to the area, a visit here is both an education, and an experience.

One shop, Yesterdays, carries cookbooks, jams, jellies, seasonings, sauces and chocolates. Another, Ashleigh's, carries top-of-the-line women's clothing, leather accessories and Brighton jewelry. Another is a year-round Christmas shop, featuring Fontanini collectables. Still another, Reflections, is geared to home and garden décor, while Little Lambs is a trendy children's boutique. Outdoor Adventures specializes in outdoor vacations.

Patti's has established a reputation for its wonderland of lights display. For the Christ-

mas Holidays over 500,000 lights are turned on, thus making this a major attraction in Kentucky.

Patti's 1880 Settlement is quite a story. It's one that started with Patti and Bill Tullar and how they started out selling hamburgers and ice cream. They then turned it into one of the finest eateries in America, with the help from their children and their families.

The Tullar's quickly recognized the importance of family, and that's what they've strived to attract.

The food, the shops, a miniature golf course, animal park, and a wedding chapel all combine to make this a must visit.

SHOPPERS INFO ?

Address:
1759 J.H. O'Bryan Avenue
Hours:
Summer Hours: 11 a.m. - 8 p.m., Sunday - Thursday
11 a.m. - 9 p.m., Friday & Saturday
Winter Hours: Closed Monday, Tuesday & Wednesday
11 a.m. - 6 p.m., Thursday, 11 a.m. - 8 p.m., Friday
11 a.m. - 8:30 p.m., Saturday, 11:00 a.m. - 6:00 p.m., Sunday
Phone:
1-888/736-2515 or 270/362-8844
Area Attractions:
Lake Barkley, Kentucky Lake

Quilt Museum
PADUCAH, KY

The official name of this incredible venue is The National Quilt Museum of the United States, although it falls under the direction of the Museum of the American Quilter's Society.

The museum is the largest of its kind in the world, and as you might expect, it has a Museum Gift Shop to match.

The shop is full of quilt books, quilt-related items and one-of-a-kind gifts. It carries over 1,000 book titles on the history of quilts, techniques, individual quilters, as well as novels and popular books related to quilting.

You'll also find a first class selection of fine hand crafted pottery, glass, fiber, wood and jewelry by more than 190 national artisans of which about 100 of them are from Kentucky. Everything sold in the shop goes to support the non-profit museum.

Beautiful stained glass windows, based on specific quilts, grace the lobby area, while a hand-carved wooden quilt hangs in the museum's conference room. Life-size statues of the Lewis and Clark Expedition occupy a portion of the front lawn connecting the Quilt Museum with local history, while at the same time providing unique artwork easily accessible to visitors regardless of the tour.

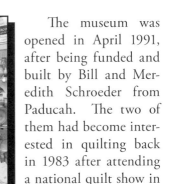

The museum was opened in April 1991, after being funded and built by Bill and Meredith Schroeder from Paducah. The two of them had become interested in quilting back in 1983 after attending a national quilt show in Tennessee. They were so impressed with the extraordinary work being created, that they wanted to help take it to another level. And they did with this beautiful facility in downtown Paducah.

When the Museum first opened it had fewer than 85 quilts, mostly on loan. Since that time these, and many others, have been donated to the museum, bringing the collection to just under 200.

There is no admission to the Gift Shop. However, there is to the Museum.

SHOPPERS INFO ?

Address:
215 Jefferson Street
Hours:
10 a.m. – 5 p.m., Monday – Saturday – Beginning April 1 – October 31, hours extend to 1 p.m. – 5 p.m. on Sunday
Phone:
270/442-8856
Area Attractions:
Flood Wall Murals, Tilghman Civil War Museum

Simon's Shoes
HENDERSON, KY

hat would a shopping book be without a shoe store? Not just any shoe store mind you, but Simon's Shoes in downtown Henderson.

One customer liked it so much she purchased 35 pairs at one time. "That's the record," says owner Bruce Simon.

It's a third generation store, begun in 1919. The store's owner liked to say that it is "Henderson's best kept secret," but in all honesty this is not the case at all. With customers driving in from Louisville, Nashville, Indianapolis, St. Louis and Bowling Green, it's pretty easy to see this store is not much of a secret.

"There are very few full-service fitting shoe stores remaining in the United States," says Simon, "but we're one of them."

Simon's specializes in a broad range of widths and sizes. Ladies shoes can be bought in 4A, 3A, 2A, B and D and sizes from 4 to 13. Brands include Munro, Magdesions, Ros Hommerson, Naturalizer, Trotters, Ugg, Finn Comfort, Naot, Birkenstock, Merrell, Clarks, Dansko, Born, Onex, New Balance, SAS and more.

Men shop Simon's almost as much as women. With sizes from 6 ½ to 17 in very narrow to extra wide, its no wonder the hard to fit know this store.

Among men's brands are Ecco, Rockport, Bostonian, Clarks, Johnston & Murphy, Florsheim, Cole Hahn, Merrell, New Balance, Red Wing and Sebago.

Simon's also has a "special"

sale room next door to their main store. The stock here is replenished weekly.

This is one of those stores that is so good that even other shoe stores buy from them when in need of a hard to find size.

"We ship by UPS all over the country," Simon says. "So if you can't find your size where you live, call and we will be more than happy to ship it to you."

SHOPPERS INFO

Address:
100 North Main Street
Hours:
9 a.m. – 5:30 p.m., Monday – Thursday
9 a.m. – 6:30 p.m., Friday
9 a.m. – 5:30 p.m., Saturday
Phone:
270/826-2341
800/826-2345
Area Attraction:
John J. Audubon State Park

In Madisonville you can look a Gift Horse in the mouth and come away smiling.

Martha Brown and Paula Milligan have one of those little shops in a small town that literally "nails it." By nailing it, I mean they have what people want at The Gift Horse. The thought process here is that if the locals love it so will visitors from other communities.

"We offer a varied selection of practical and whimsical gifts," says Paula. "And we have new items arriving everyday for every age."

Personalized merchandise is a specialty of the house. Engraved crystal, glassware, trays, Tervis Tumblers, and embroidered purses, totes and luggage are just a few of the selections.

"We can also personalize bath items, soap, candles, koozies and jewelry," Paula adds.

Bridal and baby registries are quite popular, as is the home décor area of the shop that includes prints and scrolled ironwork pieces. Wrought iron lanterns, hurricanes and jars offer some intriguing lighting options either inside or out.

The Gift Horse carries an extensive inventory of Kentucky-made products, and their specialty food items include lots of mixes, dips, soups, pastas, dressings and sauces from Gatton Farms.

Just to prove this stores versatility, they sell "tons" of country ham salad, chopped

44

country ham, whole hams and bacon.

"We have a few customers who winter in Florida," says Paula. "They call us monthly to send them the chopped country ham and country ham salad. Their Florida friends love it, too."

Obviously there are too many items to mention in a charming shop like this.

Paula says she and Martha often hear visitors from out of town say, "we wouldn't come to Madisonville without a visit to The Gift Horse."

SHOPPERS INFO

Address:
36 W. Lake Street
Hours:
9 a.m. - 5 p.m., Monday - Friday
10 a.m. - 2 p.m., Saturday
Closed Sunday
Phone:
270/825-9333
Area Attractions:
Ruby Laffoon Log Cabin

Uncle Lee's
GREENVILLE, KY

If Uncle Lee's doesn't have it, there's a good chance you don't need it.

This giant discount store in Muhlenberg County opened in 1975, in what was considered then a big store with 38,000 square feet. Today, total retail and mail order space now stands at 130,000.

Going head-to-head with the Wal-Marts, Lowe's and Bass Pro Shops of the world, Uncle Lee's has found a niche that has allowed it to remain competitive and lure shoppers from several counties in the surrounding area.

Uncle Lee's shoe department has shoes for the entire family and for all occasions. Athletic, hunting, outdoor and fashion footwear make this one stop shopping for lots of families.

Home décor includes a full-line of wallpaper and all the needed tools to make it happen. The paint is from Ace, and there's a huge department.

Plumbing, electrical, building, and lawn and garden supplies also occupy their respective areas of the store.

The furniture department takes in more than 16,000 square feet and features everything from bedroom, dining room and living room to small accent pieces.

The signature department at Uncle Lee's is their inventory of hunting and fishing equipment. The store promotes itself as offering the largest selection in Kentucky, Indiana and Tennessee. Firearms, ammunition, archery, archery accessories, game calls,

tree stands and decoys are just a sampling of what this store sells.

In the fishing and marina section you'll find rods and reels, lures, live bait and anything else you need to catch a fish.

Believe me, this store can gear you up for just about any outdoor adventure. It's one of those stores that will cause you to say a couple of things: "I've never seen anything like it," or "who would have ever thought a store like this would be located in Greenville?"

Lee Fauntleroy who opened the store, and is still active in its operation, is the stores namesake.

SHOPPERS INFO ?

Address:
820 North Main Street
Hours:
8 a.m. – 8 p.m., Monday – Saturday
10 a.m. – 6 p.m., Sunday
Phone:
270/338-5866
Area Attractions:
Everly Brothers Museum, Lake Malone

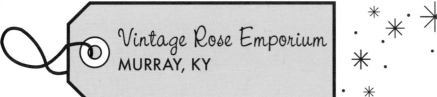

Vintage Rose Emporium
MURRAY, KY

Vintage Rose Emporium would not be out of place if it were located in Louisville or Lexington, or for that matter, Chicago or New York. But instead, it's in Murray. Not that Murray doesn't deserve a store like this, mind you, it's just that small towns often unexpectedly surprise us every now and then.

"Some consider us a small town store with a big city selection," says owner Sarah Jones.

The shop opened in 1995 in a small downtown location before moving to its current 4,000 square foot store in 2003.

Sarah, a former attorney, decided to follow her true passion when she first opened Vintage Rose.

"I had one of those 'a-ha' moments," she said in describing her decision to make a career change.

Vintage Rose has become a special place in Murray to shop for yourself or someone else.

Inventory rotates in and out, Sarah points out, thus giving customers reason to return more often.

"We take special pride in our wedding registry services, and offer a huge selection of dinner wear with most all of the national brands and many boutique and specialty brands," she adds.

Cookware, kitchen and gourmet goods usually found in much larger stores are sold here.

The stores largest product line is Vera Bradley hand-

bags and accessories, and Sarah points out her store has been recognized by the company as a signature dealer.

In 2004, Vintage Rose added "On a Personal Note Stationary" to its inventory.

"We are the only stationary shop within 150 miles who is a dealer for William Arthur and Crane, two of the most beautiful and exclusive lines in stationary today," said Sarah. "The whole room will make you want to host a party."

Custom printing for note cards, invitations, luggage tags, and all sorts of paper goods are available.

The beautiful glass atrium in the center of the store only added to the ambiance of the entire shop.

"Our customers really appreciate our exquisite free gift wrapping," Sarah continues. "And our Holiday Open House, the second weekend in November, brings shoppers in from the four state area that surrounds us."

Crabtree & Evelyn personal care products, LeCreuset Cookware, Wusthof Knives are just a hint of the quality products that can be purchased here.

SHOPPERS INFO

Address:
303 North 12th Street
Hours:
10 a.m. - 5 p.m., Monday - Friday
10 a.m. - 2 p.m., Saturday
Phone:
270/759-2100
Area Attractions:
Murray State University, Kentucky Lake

ABBEY OF GETHSEMANI	TRAPPIST, KY
ALE-8-ONE BOTTLING COMPANY	WINCHESTER, KY
... AT MARY'S	BARDSTOWN, KY
BARBARA'S	BARDSTOWN, KY
BEAUMONT INN GIFT SHOP	HARRODSBURG, KY
CHATEAU DU VIEUX CORBEAN WINERY	DANVILLE, KY
CHRISMAN MILL VINEYARD & WINERY	NICHOLASVILLE, KY
COWGIRL ATTIC	LEXINGTON, KY
DOWNTOWN LAGRANGE	LAGRANGE, KY
FIRST QUALITY MUSIC	LOUISVILLE, KY
FOR FRIENDS	LEXINGTON, KY
GLENDALE ANTIQUES	GLENDALE, KY
GREEN GABLES DOLLHOUSE SHOP	VERSAILLES, KY
HAWKS VIEW GALLERY & CAFÈ	HILLVIEW, KY
HEIRLOOMS & GRETCHEN'S	GEORGETOWN, KY
HOBBY STATION	ELIZABETHTOWN, KY
IRISH ACRES	NONESUCH, KY
JOE LEY ANTIQUES	LOUISVILLE, KY
KEENELAND GIFT SHOP	LEXINGTON, KY
KENTUCKY STATE PARK GIFT SHOPS	STATEWIDE (PAGE 34)
L.V. HARKNESS & COMPANY	LEXINGTON, KY
LEE'S GARDEN CENTER	HODGENVILLE, KY
LOUISVILLE ANTIQUE MALL	LOUISVILLE, KY
MAKER'S MARK	LORETTA, KY
MAKING ENDS MEET	SHELBYVILLE, KY
MAPLE HILL MANOR, FARM, STORE AND STUDIO	SPRINGFIELD, KY
MELLWOOD ARTS AND ENTERTAINMENT CENTER	LOUISVILLE, KY
METZGER'S COUNTRY STORE	SIMPSONVILLE, KY
MIDWAY	MIDWAY, KY
MUTH'S CANDIES	LOUISVILLE, KY
NETTIE JARVIS ANTIQUES	BLOOMFIELD, KY
POOR RICHARDS BOOKS & COMPLETELY KENTUCKY	FRANKFORT, KY
RIDGEMONT FURNITURE GALLERIES	SHEPHERDSVILLE, KY
RUTH HUNT CANDIES	MT. STERLING, KY
SHAKER VILLAGE OF PLEASANT HILL	HARRODSBURG, KY

CENTRAL REGION

SHANNON LAMPS	LEXINGTON, KY
SMITH-BERRY VINEYARD & WINERY	NEW CASTLE, KY
THE PLAID RABBIT	MT. STERLING, KY
THE SWEET SHOPPE	HODGENVILLE, KY
U.S. CAVALRY STORE	RADCLIFF, KY
WAKEFIELD-SCEARCE GALLERIES	SHELBYVILLE, KY
WILLCUTT GUITAR SHOPPE	LEXINGTON, KY

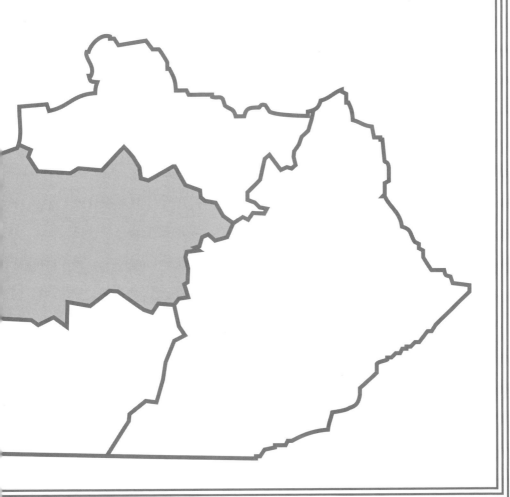

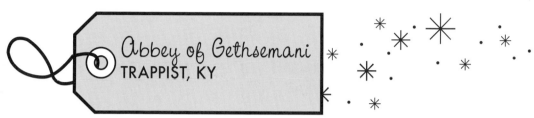

Abbey of Gethsemani
TRAPPIST, KY

*Y*ou may not expect to find the Abbey of Gethsemani in a shopping book, but when you consider that what is sold here, and through their mail orders, supports the community's livelihood, they offer some unique shopping

The Trappist cheese, fruitcake and fudge are as good as it gets, and with Gethsemani's relatively new welcome center, they have established a beautiful setting to purchase these items and more.

For those not familiar with this Trappist Monk community in Nelson County, it is someplace special regardless of a person's faith.

In 1848, forty-four Trappist monks traveled from France and made their new home in the rolling hills of Kentucky. From that time forward this has been a hardworking community. A monk's day begins at 3:15 a.m. and ends at 7:30 p.m. To a Trappist, work is a form of prayer. A balanced life of prayer, work and sacred reading, steeped in simplicity and faith, is the Trappist goal. For all their years the Trappist of Gethsemani has followed that ideal.

St. Benedict's Rule says it all: "When they live by the labor of their hands, then they are really monks."

The Abbey of Gethsemani is located just off of 31-E between Bardstown and New Haven. It is marked by a single sign not far from the small village of Culvertown. If you miss the sign, nearby Culver's Grocery can get you headed in the right direction. Ask for Louis.

Guests are welcome here, to pray, meditate in silence, or just to look around and enjoy the gift shop. It

is common to see artist sitting on a bench painting or sketching the beautiful scenery.

One thing they have done at Gethsemani is take advantage of another good Kentucky product: bourbon.

The fabulous fudge and robust fruitcakes are laced with "Kentucky finest."

The Wall Street Journal in a rating of fruit cakes, ranked Gethsemani's "best overall". The fudge, oh my goodness, comes in two varieties: chocolate bourbon and butter walnut bourbon. But it's the Trappist cheese that has become the signature item. They've been making it here since the 1940s. Four varieties are offered.

You won't soon forget a visit here, and I can guarantee you won't leave empty handed, physically or spiritually!

SHOPPERS INFO ?

Address:
3642 Monks Road
Hours:
9 a.m. - 7:30 p.m., Monday - Friday
9 a.m. - 5 p.m., Saturday
Phone:
800/549-0912
Area Attractions:
Kentucky Rail Museum, Makers Mark Distillery, My Old Kentucky Home State Park

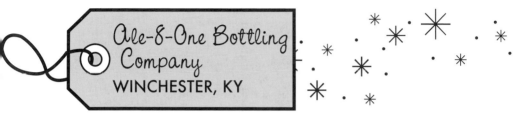

Ale-8-One Bottling Company
WINCHESTER, KY

a soft drink bottling company in a shopping book? You better believe it, especially when the drink is such an icon in Kentucky.

Ale-8-One has been bottled in Winchester since 1926, and its distinctive taste is unmatched by any other drink. Although the drink is marketed in disposables and cans, the true Ale-8 purist say it taste best in the returnable glass bottles.

G.L. Wainscott concocted the recipe, a combination of real ginger and fruit juices, and it has been passed on to several generations of the family.

The Ale-8-One Company Store is located at the plant, and it features a wide variety of apparel, keepsakes and memorabilia. Some very unique food items, with Ale-8 as a base are offered. Ale-8-One Apple Butter, a blend of cider and Ale-8, has recently been introduced.

Ale-8 sweet and spicy salsa is also a popular item.

These items, along with logo t-shirts, hoodies, caps, glassware and key chains, make a visit to the Company Store a different type of place to shop.

The popularity of Ale-8-One saw a dramatic upturn from the product's exposure in the movie *Elizabethtown*.

Director Cameron Crowe used Ale-8-One props, and lead actor Orlando Bloom wore an Ale-8 t-shirt in several scenes.

Another shot of publicity came when Winchester native Jason Epperson was a finalist and first runner

up in the Steven Spielberg reality television series, *On The Lot*. Epperson contacted Ale-8-One and had them send them some of his favorite drinks. He even wore one of the t-shirts on the show and before long other contestants and crew was also drinking Ale-8-One.

This is one of those places that are fun to visit. And besides, it's Kentucky's only soft drink. Bet you can't drink just one!

SHOPPERS INFO ?

Address:
25 Carol Road
Hours:
8:30 a.m. – 4:30 p.m., Monday – Friday
Phone:
859/744-3484
Area Attractions:
Bluegrass Heritage Museum

...at Mary's
BARDSTOWN, KY

Don't walk into ...at Mary's with a frown on. Don't walk into ...at Mary's in a bad mood. Because if you do they won't last long.

...At Mary's is full of cheerful, bright colors and possesses an energy that will quickly turn anyone's bad day into a good one.

Mary Carey and her husband Dennis, back in 2004, took a 200-year-old building in the heart of downtown Bardstown and turned it into an outstanding place to shop.

"Even if you don't plan on buying anything its just a fun store to go in and see what they have new," said one local shopper.

"I wanted to put my marketing and business degree to work," Mary pointed out. "I needed an avenue to express myself."

And she has done it up right!

Beautiful art, antiques, made-to-order floral arrangements, custom framing, and a bevy of unusual gifts all add to the experience of visiting ...at Mary's.

In this shop it doesn't take long to realize that Mary has an eye for art. Her photography and framing background has carried over to her providing an expertise her customer can count on in finding just the art with just the right frame that is just the right size. It's not always as easy as it seems.

Mary's store is full of stuff:

Louisville Stoneware, Lolita hand-painted martini and wine glasses. These are the ones with drink recipes printed on the bottom of each glass and presented in a beautiful cylinder box.

Black leather club chairs, iron beds, oriental rugs, eclectic arm chairs, cherry inlaid desk, and dining tables are displayed throughout.

Just when you think you have her shop figured out, up pops a display for bedding, pajamas, robes, bath towels, linens, jewelry, and tea and, of course, cook books.

…At Mary's will put a smile on your face even if you don't want it.

SHOPPERS INFO ?

Address:
116 N. Third
Hours:
10 a.m. 6 p.m., Monday – Saturday
Closed on Sunday with the exception of special events
Phone:
502/350-9009
Area Attractions:
Distillers, My Old Kentucky Home, Stephen Foster Outdoor Drama

Barbara's
BARDSTOWN, KY

*B*ardstown has long been noted as a fun place to visit. Its downtown area is conducive to parking and being able to cover an assortment of interesting shops and restaurants, without having to move your car from one spot to another.

North Third Street, near the centrally located old court house, might be considered the "main drag" when it comes to shopping. However, one of the town's best surprises of all is Barbara's, a nearby upscale shop at 109 West Flaget Avenue.

For well over two decades Barbara Mattingly and her business associate, Harriett Ballard, have taken great pride in building a reputation among the locals as one fine place to shop.

Barbara's is not just a shop to buy for others but one that presents high end furniture and accessories for homeowners interested in quality.

Although the store might appear to be heavy in furniture, Barbara will quickly tell you "we're not a furniture store."

"We display the furniture we have in a home-like presentation so customers can get an idea of how it might look with certain accessories," she offers.

The store has a great reputation for its interior design from in-home consultation that includes complete remodeling to painting to floor coverings.

Barbara's is one of those

"walk-around-and-stand-back-and-look stores." An upstairs area includes several areas of displays.

Couches, chairs, bedrooms, dining tables, lamps, pictures, furniture and accessories for the nursery are all offered in this wonderful shop.

SHOPPERS INFO

?

Address:
109 West Flaget Avenue
Hours:
9 a.m. - 4 p.m., Monday - Friday
10 a.m. - 3 p.m., Saturday
Phone:
502/348-2519
Area Attractions:
Stephen Foster Outdoor Drama, Distilleries

Beaumont Inn Gift Shop
HARRODSBURG, KY

Some people might think the Beaumont Inn in Harrodsburg is only for eating and overnighting. Add one more thing to the list. Shopping!

The best way to describe hospitality guru Duncan Hines' favorite place to eat in all of Kentucky is country elegance. It's not "fancy smancy", nor is it flip-flops and a tank top. Perhaps like baby bear soup – it's just right.

The dining room and lodging accommodations are superlative. And so is the Beaumont Inn Gift Shop that dates back to around 1940.

Anne Belle Goddard and her daughter, Pauline Goddard Dedman, opened the shop realizing the potential of the hotel's guests buying something for someone left at home.

Originally housed in one room, over the years the Gift Shop has expanded to four rooms. The main room and silver room are original to the Inn, while the pine room and back room are enclosed porches that wrap around the outside.

"The advantage of having four rooms, besides allowing us to have more merchandise, is it gives the shop a nice stroll through atmosphere," says Helen Dedman, who along with husband Chuck runs the Beaumont Inn.

Helen says their goal is to offer merchandise that one does not see everywhere.

"This is a challenge," she says. "Because of the 'big box stores', internet shopping and shops everywhere, but through travels and long hours at market we seem to have found a niche."

One of those niches is the "men's corner" with all kinds of gift ideas for that difficult-to-buy-for man on your list. Weddings, babies, and even pets all have their space in this shop. And it wouldn't be a first class gift shop this near Lexington if it didn't carry a collection of offerings for the horse enthusiasts.

The Beaumont Inn carries an array of seasonal gifts, but they have earned a reputation for their Christmas collectibles and decorations. An assortment of their very own Beaumont Inn signature items has a section of their own. Among them are the green tomato relish and corn meal battercake mix.

Helen says the gifts her shop sells are made even more distinctive by the free-gift wrap they offer.

"We wrap in beautiful paper then tie it up with a handmade bow of three or four different colors of ribbon to compliment the paper," she says. "I've heard the comment at several gift giving occasions, oh, that is from the Beaumont Inn, you can tell by the wrapping."

An added bonus here is a staff that is not only helpful, but knowledgeable about what they sell.

SHOPPERS INFO

Address:
638 Beaumont Inn Drive
Hours:
Wednesday – Saturday, during lunch and dinner
Sunday during Brunch buffet
Phone:
859/734-3381
Area Attractions:
Fort Harrod, Shakertown

Chateau du Vieux Corbean Winery
DANVILLE, KY

From the beginning lets cut down on any confusion of the names here. Chateau du Vieux Corbean is the French name of the winery on the Old Crow Inn Farm, and the name translates to "house of old crow."

Since 2000, the Brousseau family has been in the wine business, making approximately 6,000 gallons of wine each year.

The marquee structure on the farm is a beautiful stone house, known as the Old Crow Inn that dates to 1780, and is listed on the National Registry as the oldest stone house west of the Alleghenies.

"When we decided to get into the wine business," says Linda Brousseau, "We decided as a family to do it right, and that included our winery building."

And first class it is. Built from the cellar up, its stone work mimics the "main house" with hand-laid stone. The inside is equally impressive with beautiful warm tones of dark wood and wine cabinets to match.

There, another unexpected dimension to the visit, is that Linda was a full-time professional potter/artist for over 30 years, so her influence of art and special crafts are evident in the winery.

Youngest daughter, Dominique is the winemaker, and recognized as the youngest in Kentucky, beginning at age 22. She is one of three women winemakers in Kentucky.

Dominique, early on, learned the craft by helping an older brother André, an amateur winemaker. That led her to California for further instruction at the University of California at Davis. That was followed by an apprenticeship with Jerry Kushner, the oldest winemaker in the state, at Broad Run Winery.

The gift shop and tasting room are fun. Of course you can sample various wines before deciding. Linda's pottery, art, and seasonal items such as pumpkins and vegetables offer an experience for just about everyone. For those who don't want to buy anything, there are some neat trails that wander through the woods and fields, perfect for hiking.

CENTRAL

SHOPPERS INFO

Address:
471 Stanford Road
Hours:
11 a.m. - 6 p.m., Monday – Saturday
Closed Sunday
Phone:
859/236-1808
Area Attractions:
Pioneer Playhouse, Constitution Square, Center College

We are reminded quite often the storied role bourbon plays in our state's history. There are all kinds of reasons Kentucky bourbon taste good. But there are also lots of reasons Kentucky wines taste good, too.

Chrisman Mills Winery, in Jessamine County, is the oldest operating winery in central Kentucky, and the county lays claim to being home to the first commercial vineyard in the United States in 1799!

The vineyard and winery is owned by Denise Nelson and husband Dr. Chris Nelson, who is a master winemaker. Long before they planted their several varieties of rooted cuttings back in 1997, they traveled extensively throughout the Midwest visiting numerous grape-growing regions similar to the conditions of their central Kentucky property.

"We wanted to determine what grape varieties were best suited to our soil and climate," offered Denise.

Chrisman Mill is full of photo ops. A cobblestone trail that leads to the winery takes visitors past a trickling waterfall. Opening the French doors of the winery releases an aroma of homemade wine breads.

As visitors slowly sip and taste the various wines offered up, they get added enjoyment from the beautiful hand-painted murals and original art that clings to the rooms' walls. A gift shop is close by.

Chrisman Mill Vineyards has been recognized with several national awards. Recently

they were awarded "Top 10 Best Buy in the United States," and over the years have won over 30 medals for their wines, including a recent gold on the First Vineyard Reserve, a dry red wine from a blend of Kentucky grown Chambourcin and Cabernet Franc.

The Winery also has a first class café that opens for lunch. The Tuscan cafe serves up an authentic Tuscan cuisine that includes an appetizer, entrée with accompaniments, dessert and beverage. Lunch is served 11:30 a.m. – 2:30 p.m. during winery hours.

Address:
2385 Chrisman Mill Road
Hours:
11 a.m. - 5 p.m., Tuesday - Friday
11 a.m. - 6 p.m., Saturday
Closed Sunday & Monday
Phone:
859/881-5007
Area Attractions:
Camp Nelson Civil War Park

Cowgirl Attic
LEXINGTON, KY

*K*aren Payne started riding horses at the age of five. Because of that she has always considered herself a cowgirl.

Over the years she had been in the business of pedaling antiques and old house parts, so when she decided to open her 5,000 square foot warehouse/store, the name was a no-brainer.

Cowgirl Attic is stacked with architectural antiques, light fixtures, fireplace mantles, doors, bath fixtures, hardware, stained glass, stationary, ornamental iron, garden elements, stone, bricks, ironwork, weathervanes, furniture, beams, flooring and much, much more.

"I collect vintage cowgirl things," says Karen. "And since we are in horse country, we carry a large selection of related items."

Those items include a diversified selection of horse, cowboy, cowgirl, western and ranch items for decorating a farm, house, cabin or even a restaurant.

Cowgirl Attic has assembled lots and lots of local salvage, but don't be surprised when you see merchandise from Europe, China, Egypt and Mexico.

Karen has assembled, for sure, a unique store, and for the last 11 years she has not only been selling, but buying as well.

"I am always interested in purchasing salvage," she points out. "I like 100-year-

old homes, old barns, old cabins, claw foot tubs, pedestal sinks, door knobs and old windows."

Cowboy Attic considers itself an urban recycler. Their literature emphasizes they do not promote the destruction and removal of historic buildings, but offer an opportunity to preserve and reuse the architectural details that are of quality and historical significance. This they say helps conserve and keeps usable building materials out of landfills.

SHOPPERS INFO

?

Address:
1535 Delaware Avenue
Hours:
10 a.m. - 5 p.m., Monday & Tuesday
10 a.m. - 6 p.m., Wednesday - Friday
10 a.m. - 5 p.m., Saturday
1 p.m. - 4 p.m., Sunday
Phone:
859/225-3876
Area Attractions:
Horses

Downtown LaGrange
LAGRANGE, KY

nyone who has ever visited or just passed through downtown LaGrange will never forget it, because there's a good chance you've had to stop and wait for a train to pass through, as it runs smack-dab down the center of Main Street.

If you're anywhere near the tracks you know it starts with a low rumble. Then you hear the bells. And suddenly the ground beneath your feet begins to tremble, like, perhaps an earthquake.

For first time visitors it's an unusual experience. But for those who live and work in LaGrange it's all a part of life in this very charming town, as up to 30 trains a day pass through.

The town's downtown area is full, on both sides of the street, of over 20 shops that sell antiques, crafts and collectibles. With a handful of eateries nearby, this is a place you can visit and easily spend several hours

browsing, shopping and entertaining yourself in the delightful surroundings.

The Treasured Child Toy Store, reputed to be the largest privately owned toy store in Kentucky, is one of the district's marquee shops.

An old 1830 federal-style building houses the Christmas in Kentucky shop. It's a shop that gets visitors in the holiday mood regardless of what time of year it is.

Karen's Book Barn and Java Stop is very popular for visitors and locals alike. It's one of those places that almost screams at you to slooow down, munch on a locally baked muffin, sip a cup of coffee, and look at all of those books. They even have a section where customers can purchase used books by the pound.

The 1887 corner store is a local gem of a place. And so are their unique gifts. From Crabtree & Evelyn to the finest of linens, this is a must visit.

Gallery 104, one might say, is an uptown art gallery in historic downtown. It fits and it works!

LaGrange also offers an interesting ghost walking tour, and seasonally a Farmers Market. You'll want to call ahead to verify times.

SHOPPERS INFO

Address:
Main Street
Hours:
Varies from store to store
Phone:
502/243-9353 or 866/829-0578
Area Attractions:
Horse Farms, Yew-dell Gardens

First Quality Music
LOUISVILLE, KY

When it comes to stringed musical instruments, the name says it all: First Quality Music.

First started in 1970 as a hobby out of his basement, Bill Sullivan and his two sons, Jeff and Eric have built this store into one of the finest music stores in the country.

"My dad played the banjo on his lunch hour when he worked at General Electric," says son Jeff. "He made pieces and parts for banjos and it just took off."

From a backyard workshop and now to an 18,000 square foot facility that employees some 30 people, First Quality Music is THE store when it comes to any musical instrument with strings. A full-line, full-service operation, that sells, has a call center/mail order, and manufactures, make this store extra special.

"We build the Sullivan banjo and also some manufacturing for Gibson," says Jeff. "We are the largest in Kentucky and one of the largest in the nation when it comes to dealing in Martin, Gibson and Fender guitars."

You won't find a horn section in this store, only strings. And for the novice, the correct term for stringed instruments besides the fiddle family is fretted. First Quality Music prides itself in high-end merchandise. They are also proud of the fact that all of their salespeople are musicians.

"They can pretty much answer any question asked of them," says Jeff. "If they can't, we have someone in the store that can."

Guitars, banjos, mandolins, violins, upright bass, acoustics, sound systems, it's all here, with guitars ranging in price from $500 to $15,000.

Another element that makes this place so special is the lessons it gives. Nine teachers oversee 250 students a week at the facility. Some of these students are learning just for the fun and pleasure of it, while a few just might reach a level of some of the so-called big names who have visited the store. Over the years Bluegrass legends Earl Scruggs, Ricky Skaggs, Sam Bush, Jimmy Martin and J.D. Crow have all stopped by this fantastic store.

SHOPPERS INFO

Address:
7006 Trade Port Drive
Hours:
10 a.m. - 6 p.m., Monday - Friday
10 a.m. - 5 p.m., Saturday
Phone:
1/800-635-2021
Area Attractions:
Six Flags Park, Muhammad Ali Center, Churchill Downs Museum

For Friends
LEXINGTON, KY

Sharri Greer and Jill McCarty were friends when they opened For Friends in 1986 as a small gift and accessories shop. But apparently they didn't realize just how many friends they had, because today they operate a 10,000 square foot store in the Idle House Shopping Center on Richmond Road.

Design services that include the store's line of furniture, fabric and wallpaper, window treatments, bedding and upholstery have become extremely popular. Megan Green and Emily Dexter have even had some of their projects featured on *HGTV* and in magazines *Better Homes and Gardens* and *Kentucky Home and Garden*.

For Friends offers a wide variety of artwork as well as antique reproduction furniture, and one section of the store is dedicated to the baby nursery.

Dinnerware such as Vietri and Mariposa compliment the fine china

lines by Herend and Mottahedeh! Hadley Pottery and Louisville Stoneware, two Kentucky-made products, are also sold here.

Pillows, lamps, rugs and silk floral arrangements only add to the enjoyment of shopping here. The store lays claim to being one of the largest sellers of Vera Bradley in the United States.

There are lots of gift stores. They're everywhere. But it is the total package store like For Friends that separate it from the others. This is a shop that keeps pace with trends and customers wants and needs. Its in-store displays change frequently in order to present a fresh look depending on the season of the year.

It truly is a fun place to shop.

SHOPPERS INFO

Address:
869 East High Street
Hours:
10 a.m. – 6 p.m., Monday – Saturday
12:30 p.m. – 5 p.m., Sunday
Phone:
859/268-2576
1-800/676-4063
Area Attractions:
Horse Farms, Keeneland Race Course

Glendale Antiques
GLENDALE, KY

If someone had not been to Glendale in a long, long time they would probably think it still looks the same. There are still a number of residential and commercial buildings, and several times a day trains rumble and thunder through the heart of the small town. In all probability they'll like what they see.

The same can be said for first-time visitors to the charming antique community that over the years has re-invented itself into a shopping destination from several states.

Located a couple of miles off I-65, 14 miles south of E-town, this is one place you can tie up a good part of the day moving from one unique shop to another. You can take a break, if needed, at Sweet Dreams Old Fashioned Ice Cream Parlor and Sweet Shop. I don't need to go into detail what they sell. Use your imagination.

Glendale is one busy place. With over 14 shops, several hundred dealers are represented here.

True Kentucky carries all Kentucky-made products from gourmet foods to antiques; Green Top Antiques has over 66 booths and 35 showcases inside; Bennie's Barn Antique Mall has three floors of antiques displayed; Glendale Antique Mall represents 45 separate dealers; The Raspberry Shop sells jewelry, home décor, and, of course, antiques; Where Dreams Come True is a little different with its fine art, jewelry and military items; Thru the Grapevine offers French linens, gourmet kitchen stuff, Vera Bradley and unique soaps; Once Upon A Country Road features painted furniture; The Sisters Shop deals in collectible bears, specialty foods and coffees;

Seasons of Elegance is a boutique. Among the many items they carry are sterling silver, sweaters, hats and scarves; The Village Shoppe highlights a collection of lamps as well as lace, candles, quilts and furniture; The Side Track Antique Mall houses 20 separate shops under one roof.

Glendale is perfect for taking advantage of the meandering sidewalks as you explore your way through an abundance of arts, furniture, glassware, antiques, collectibles and crafts.

At the end of the day, if you've planned ahead and made reservations, you can overnight at Petticoat Junction Bed & Breakfast, just a block or so off the main drag.

There's probably not a town this small in Kentucky that has two outstanding eateries like Glendale does.

Tony York's on Main offers a fine dining experience in a laid back atmosphere, while across the tracks on the other side of the street is The Whistle Stop Restaurant, a "southern cooking" delight.

The highlight of the year is the annual Glendale Crossing Festival the third Saturday in October. Over 600 booths display wares, and crowds number over 20,000.

SHOPPERS INFO

Address:
Hwy. 222, I-65, exit 86
Hours:
Open 7 days a week – although some shops are closed on Monday
Phone:
Glendale Merchants
270/369-6188
Area Attractions:
Coca-Cola Museum, Civil War History, Lincoln's Birthplace,
Claudia's Tea Room in Sonora

CENTRAL

Green Gables Dollhouse Shop
VERSAILLES, KY

There's usually a good story behind most names for a business, and Green Gables Dollhouse Shop is no exception.

In the beginning owner Missy Rogers had named her business after her daughter, Rachel.

"After she grew up she didn't like having a retail business named after her," says Missy. "I had always loved the old *Anne of Green Gables* series of books that were published around 1900, and since the dollhouses was often so old-fashioned I decided on the name Green Gables."

She has always had an interest in dollhouses and miniatures, and it was only enhanced when an old family friend left his own mother's collection to Missy upon his death.

"He didn't have any children and it dated back to 1870," she added. "I enjoyed working on the house, and finally my business developed from a hobby that I have practiced for 35 years."

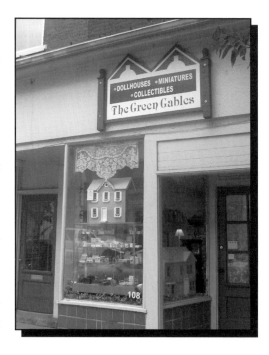

Missy's first shop was actually in nearby Lexington. She closed it and began working out of her home for a while before opening her present location on the Main Street in Versailles.

Here customers come from all over Kentucky and they love it!

Missy says her shop is for little girls four to 94.

"It sounds corny, but one of the pleasures of being

in this kind of business is seeing the enjoyment people get out of creating something that often becomes an heirloom."

She has been in the dollhouse business for some 25 years and says she now sees customers in their twenties having a great time re-decorating dollhouses Santa Claus brought them when they were ten.

Any hobby can be expensive, but Green Gables carries an inventory that can be managed by just about any pocketbook.

For example, a 3-piece hand painted bathroom set goes for $295. But there's also one in ceramic for $18.

And how about the dollhouses themselves?

The kits begin at about $40 and go all the way up to over $1,000.

Missy has a studio where she custom finishes dollhouses for customers as well as creating dollhouses she ships all over the country.

SHOPPERS INFO

Address:
108 North Main Street
Hours:
10 a.m. - 5 p.m., Tuesday - Saturday
Thursday night open until 7 p.m.
Phone:
859/873-5086
Area Attractions:
Horse Farms

CENTRAL

Hawks View
Gallery & Café
HILLVIEW, KY

A visit to this beautiful shop offers up the best of both worlds. First class shopping in a café atmosphere.

Hawks View is a glass art gallery where visitors can watch glass blowers do their craft. The shop features primarily hand-blown glass created in the on-site studio. The large observation windows allow you to watch and appreciate the artists as they delicately handle, twirl and swirl the hot, molten glass. Years of experience allow them to process a combination of sand, silica, soda ash and limestone into pieces of art.

The inspiration behind Hawks View is Celeste North (she goes by the name of Bernie), who opened the business in 1996. Today, along with her sister Therese Hutton-Crump, they have turned this unique business into a must stop – to shop, and now to eat.

"Bernie" has her work in over 1,500 galleries in all 50 states, as well as Canada and Europe. She has appeared in art shows from Florida to Colorado to Maryland, and her work has been purchased by numerous celebrities. Among them, gymnast Cathy Rigby, singer Naomi Judd, basketball player Michael Jordon, and one of the original members of the Temptations. She has done several major commissions over the years.

She says she draws her inspiration for designs from the strengths and subtleties of the four historic elements of nature: earth, wind, fire and water. Her work includes a wide range of functional pieces, abstract forms, water fountains, chandeliers, and nature based sculptures.

The gallery also features works from several other American artists to include nature photography, metal, leather, fabric and pottery. Many of the pieces are functional.

There are seven glass blowers who craft their wares here, and usually they can be seen from 10 a.m. to 4 p.m., Monday through Thursday, and 10:30 a.m. to 10 p.m. on Friday. If you're coming to the shop just to see them you may want to call ahead. There's even counter space in front of one of the windows where patrons can eat while watching the unique show on the other side. And if the shop is crowded there's a closed-circuit feed that can be seen on an elevated T.V. screen.

Many of the pieces are almost breathtaking, and prices range from $10 to more than $5,000 for certain works. By all means make sure you see the "slightly imperfect section." There's some great buys here.

SHOPPERS INFO

Address:
170 Carter Avenue- Take I-65 South from Louisville to Brooks Road, Exit #121. Turn left on Brooks Road, and then left at the light on Bluelick Road and right on Carter Avenue. On your left, just 0.7 miles from I-65 exit.

Hours:
10 a.m. – 5 p.m., Monday – Thursday, 10 a.m. – 10 p.m. – Friday
9 a.m. – 10 p.m. – Saturday; Lunch, Monday – Friday, 11 a.m. – 3:30 p.m.,
Dinner, Friday & Saturday, 5 p.m. – 10 p.m.

Phone:
502/955-1010

Area Attractions:
Bernheim Forest

This is one of those little stores that really pack a wallop. Pow! And you've got to love the interesting name that came about of combining two businesses into one.

At Heirlooms & Gretchen's in downtown Georgetown there's a lot going on, particularly with stained glass, antique lamps, dollhouses and antiques.

The antiques are stashed here and there all over the store, and owner Gretchen Soards readily admits that she is not very knowledgeable when it comes to antiques. "Because we're not," she says. "People can find some pretty good bargains, and they tend to come back to look periodically. We don't even pretend to compete with the 'antique district' here in Georgetown."

She doesn't have to. The uniqueness of her store has a customer base and a good word-of-mouth reputation.

And about those dollhouses. Some of those are antiques, especially the metal ones, dating back to the 30s and 40s. They even have accessories from that period. Their new modern dollhouses are fully furnished with some of the thousands of accessories they keep in stock.

The lamp section of the store stocks more than 100 different glass shades, as well as 75 different chimneys.

"We even have had a couple from Puerto Rico in our shop twice," Gretchen said. "They heard about our shop and were in Cincinnati, so they made a side trip here."

Make no mistake about it, however, stained glass is the major part of the business.

"People seem to enjoy seeing what we do," she adds. "At any given time we may have a 1800s piece on the table for restoration, or a new transom or side light commissioned piece in progress."

Gretchen is proud of the fact that more than 200 students have taken part in the store's stained glass class.

"We have some who really work with glass," she said, "and have far surpassed what we taught them."

Gretchen is quick to point out that husband Roy, staff members Anne Quigley and Kathy Jordan are a big part of the store's success. She also allows that Maggie, "our Australian Shepherd mix, now watches the door and greets customers instead of chasing cattle."

SHOPPERS INFO **?**

Address:
136 W. Main Street
Hours:
10 a.m. – 5 p.m., Monday – Saturday
1 p.m. – 5 p.m., Sunday
Phone:
502/863-2538
Area Attractions:
Toyota Plant

Hobby Station
ELIZABETHTOWN, KY

If ever a person was born to own and operate the Hobby Station it is Timothy Coyle. You see, the store places a big emphasis on model railroading and toy trains in general, and Timothy grew up on a farm in Hardin County next to the Louisville & Nashville Railroad track. As a baby he would imitate train sounds while standing in his baby crib.

It was only natural that he became an avid train watcher, and witnessed L & N's transition from steam to diesel power.

"I also saw the vanishing of the great L & N passenger trains such as the Pan American, Hummingbird, and the South Wind," Timothy offers.

As he collected old trains and toy trains he was astounded at the lack of information on the L & N as a hobby source.

When he decided to become involved in the hobby industry, he set out to emphasize the L & N and affiliate railroads in his store. With very few L & N trains available, he decided to have custom models made with L & N graphics. Now he stocks engines, boxcars, hopper cars, cabooses, passenger cars and billboard refrigeration cars.

In the past, what the Hobby Station now sells could only be purchased by mail order or model train shows. Quite possibly Timothy Coyle has the largest collection of L & N train models in the country.

Although trains are big at the Hobby Station, they are not the only thing sold here. He specializes in N, HO and O gauges.

Model kits of cars, trucks, ships, planes and military models; die cast models; 12-inch collectables, military, movies, horror figures and hand-painted metal toy soldiers; radio control planes, trucks, helicopters and boats; and the very popular wooden infant toys are all stocked here.

This is one neat store.

Paints, puzzles, rockets, games, hobby supplies, antique toys, books and magazines, that are hobby related, line the shelves.

This specialty store is one you'll definitely want to keep in mind for that special person. And it doesn't have to be a child either. There's something for every age, boys and girls, men and women.

Thank goodness Timothy grew up next to a railroad track.

SHOPPERS INFO ?

Address:
200 Sycamore Street, Suite 111
Hours:
11 a.m. - 7 p.m., Monday - Saturday
12 noon - 5 p.m., Sunday
Phone:
270/737-2000
Area Attractions:
Coca Cola Museum, Gold Vault, Glendale Antiques

a t Irish Acres you can have your cake and eat it too. The best of both worlds are in the 1930-something former elementary school building.

When you walk past the antebellum-like columns, and through the front door, you come face-to-face with a world-class antique gallery. To tell you the truth it's almost overwhelming, in a good sort of way.

While twinkling lights and sparkling chandeliers add an emphasis to the grandeur of the place, what's really impressive is the attention to detail. The precise artistic arrangements of the furniture, art, silver, crystal, jewelry, glassware, clothing, and Christmas ornaments, makes every turn a pleasant surprise.

The Horrigan family, dad Arch and daughters Jane DeLauter and Emilee McCauley, have spent more than two decades turning Irish Acres into a destination.

The icing on the cake is the Glitz tearoom located in the basement's

former school cafeteria. This space has been transformed into an elegant, classy, yet somewhat gaudy, dining room that would not be out of place in Paris, New York City or San Francisco. What a place to eat after a couple hours of browsing.

The collection of merchandise hails from four continents and there's something to fit any size pocketbook or checkbook, whichever is the case. Whether it's a pair of vintage earrings for $5 or a 200-year-old mahogany corner cupboard with shell carving for $38,500, there's something here for you.

Jane and Emilee are both as delightful as the business they run, and as graduates of the Atlanta School of Interior Design, they have plans for an art gallery and English-style garden.

The beautiful horse country of Woodford County only adds to the enjoyment of the visit. The twisting, winding, two lane road demands that you slow down and enjoy the beauty before you.

SHOPPERS INFO ?

Address:
4205 Fords Mill Road
Hours:
10 a.m. – 5 p.m., Tuesday – Saturday
Opens on St. Patrick's Day and closes the last day of December
Phone:
859/873-7235
Area Attractions:
Horse Farms

Joe Ley Antiques
LOUISVILLE, KY

There's not anything else like this store, anywhere. Joe Ley Antiques is an architect's and builder's dream. Regardless of what you need in the way of restoration or something old, there's a great chance you can find it in this old three-story, 1890 Hiram Roberts School.

Joe Ley, even though a retail store, has become a tourist attraction over the years, as thousands and thousands of people visit to browse and poke around. If you listen carefully you'll hear others say, "I used to have one of those." That's why this place is so popular; Joe Ley now has what all of us used to have.

"I like to collect the odd-ball stuff," says Joe Ley, who has been in this salvage collecting business for 42 years. The last 29 have been at his present location.

Ley has traveled all over the country, literally buying up old houses and buildings just for the windows, ironwork, staircases, columns, moldings, hardware, bathroom fixtures, fences, gates, fountains, shutters and on and on and on.

The store is full of antique toys, unique signs, carousel animals, stained glass, crystal, chandeliers, carriage lamps, glass, brass and silver.

"Over the years some of our collections have gone into hundreds of restaurants across the country," Ley

says. "And several country music video, movie scenes and commercials have been filmed here."

This unique place has also been written up in national publications like *House Beautiful* and *Travel and Leisure.*

For the first time visitor, Joe Ley Antiques can almost be overwhelming. You wonder how they keep up with it all.

SHOPPERS INFO

Address:
615 E. Market Street
Hours:
8:30 a.m. – 5 p.m., Tuesday – Saturday
Closed Sunday & Monday
Phone:
502/583-4017
Area Attractions:
Churchill Downs Museum, Belle of Louisville, Muhammad Ali Museum, Riverfront

Keeneland Gift Shop
LEXINGTON, KY

$\mathcal{M}$ost of us probably wouldn't think of making the Gift Shop at Keeneland Race Course a destination for shopping. Oh sure, there's a good possibility you might do a walk through or even pick up something or other if you were there to watch the ponies run, but just to go there to shop?

You betcha!

The gift shop is one winner you'll have for sure.

For those of you who think Keeneland is just a race track, you should also know it is a major seller of thoroughbred race horses. The annual Keeneland Sales is considered by most to be among the most prestigious of its type in the world. Each year this beautiful venue, which dates back to 1936, attracts horse racing enthusiasts from more than 40 countries, six continents and nearly every state, to buy, sell, race and enjoy some of the sports equine stars.

The Keeneland Gift Shop

As classy as the Keeneland grandstands, grounds, and sales arena are, the gift shop holds its own.

Reputed to be quite possibly the world's finest equine gift shop, it attracts a discriminating clientele with impeccable taste. It sells high quality, luxurious brands from Longchamp, Water-

ford, Barbour and Vineyard Vines, Carrera y Carrera, and Caerleon Jewelry.

The gift shop even has its own signature Keeneland Collection by Lady Primrose, featuring fragrances, and personal care products. This line has been created exclusively for the Keeneland Gift Shop, so it's for sure you won't find this anywhere else.

An impressive collection of distinctive apparel, art prints, jewelry, memorabilia, one-of-a-kind home accessories, and beautiful distinctive logo-wear, make this a must visit.

The Keeneland Gift Shop is open throughout the year, even when no races are scheduled.

SHOPPERS INFO

Address:
4201 Versailles Road – Keeneland
Hours:
9 a.m. – 4 p.m., Monday – Saturday
Extended hours during race meets, horse sales and holidays
Phone:
859/288-4185
Area Attraction:
Horse Farms

L.V. Harkness & Company
LEXINGTON, KY

*E*very business usually has a story behind it, and L.V. Harkness & Company in downtown Lexington is no exception.

Let's begin by pointing out that this is a store of choice among discriminating shoppers.

Now for the story.

In 1869, at the young age of 19, Lamon Vanderburg Harkness, with a $500 stake from his father launched a career in land and cattle. His passion for some of the finer things in life became evident as he began to collect silver, crystal, boats and horses.

L.V., over time, had become a rather large shareholder in Standard Oil Company, a company co-founded by his father.

In 1891, L.V. purchased Walnut Hall Stock Farm near Lexington. Now with a driven passion for horses, he set out to transform Walnut Hall into the foremost standard bred breeding and racing establishment in the world. With an uncompromising taste and a keen eye for bloodlines, his achievements in breeding of the standard bred was widely recognized.

L.V. was also a worldwide traveler, even sailing around the globe on his yacht, *Wakiva*. As one might suspect he accumulated fine objects to adorn his homes.

Today, his great-granddaughter, Meg Jewett, shares his love of standard breeds, fine art, and even his spirit for adventure.

She, too, travels the world in search of world treasures to bring back and share through L.V. Harkness & Company.

The business opened in 2000 primarily as a store with the finest of gifts and couture for the table. Over the years, however, it has expanded to include corporate and executive gifting, on-site personalization of silver, glass, crystal, leather, wood, acrylic, and marble. An extensive Home Collection of fine furniture, lighting, floor and wall coverings, fabric, bed linens, towels, and a full-service bridal registry.

One step inside of this wonderful store and you quickly see why they say "our hallmark is quality," and an abundance of equine related gifts only add to making this shopping experience uniquely Kentucky.

SHOPPERS INFO ?

Address:
531 West Short Street
Hours:
10 a.m. - 6 p.m., Monday - Friday
10 a.m. - 5 p.m., Saturday
Also by appointment
Phone:
866/225-7474
Area Attractions:
Horses

Lee's Garden Center
HODGENVILLE, KY

What a pleasant surprise when this top-shelf garden center just seems to appear out of nowhere on the outskirts of Hodgenville on Highway 31-E. This is a gardener's dream!

Flowering vegetables, shrubs, trees, bulbs, baskets, mulch, bird houses, yard furniture and water ponds are displayed in a most pleasant setting.

Scott and Robin Lee began growing plants to wholesale back in 1984, growing as many as 50,000 flats yearly. Then in 1995, they went retail when they opened at their current location.

In 2000, they built a log cabin, and ever since, the Lee's have been adding to and bringing in more and more inventory that appeals to do-it-yourself gardens as well as commercial.

"We now feature water gardening with a parade of ponds in July," says Scott Lee, in talking about the store's several displays as well as how-to instructions.

Lee's Garden Center has become an agricultural learning center for over 2,000 school kids each October.

When business really starts popping, the Lee children, Judd and Ashley, pitch in after school, and Scott's mom is pretty much a fixture in the store during the week. Like so many businesses in this book, family plays a big roll in its success.

Scott says there's a philosophy his family has when it comes to the business. "If you're not changing you're go-

ing backwards," he offers. "Nothing stays the same very long."

To prove his point, he says they want to add a bed and breakfast to the business, as well as increase the retail area dedicated to grown-local food.

"We plan to expand our vegetable production that we sell retail," he adds. "And then add a processing room on our adjoining property."

Lee's draws customers from several counties in the region. A visit here and you will quickly understand why they sell over 3,000 hanging baskets, and more than 20,000 flats of wave petunias.

This is a fun place to shop for bedding plants, trees, fresh produce, gardening supplies, custom potting, garden gifts and even antiques.

SHOPPERS INFO ?

Address:
1918 Bardstown Road (31-E)
Hours:
8 a.m. – 5 p.m., Monday – Saturday
Closed Sunday
Phone:
270/358-9897
Area Attractions:
Lincoln's Birthplace, Lincoln's Boyhood Home

Louisville Antique Mall
LOUISVILLE, KY

It promotes itself as "one of the oldest and largest antique malls in the country." And who's to say it's not.

The Louisville Antique Mall has over 200 qualified dealers that occupy space in this five story building that became their "new home" about a year ago after a quarter of a century of doing business on Goss Avenue.

Even though the Mall is located facing Broadway, the "main entrance" is in the rear, just off the alley between Campbell and Logan streets.

"We closed the Broadway entrance because of no parking availability," said owner, Denise Golden. "We have two lots behind the building so it just made sense."

Denise has owned the Antique Mall since 1995, and after searching for a new location over several years she decided the 1920s art deco-style building would suit her just fine. Before she moved her business in, the building had some history of its own, making tubs, sinks, and toilets under the American Standard name.

The Mall's street level features a number of glass cases displaying silver and estate jewelry, and booths with period furniture. The other four floors, of course, have booths and lots of vintage clothing, linens, glassware, china, silver, books, Victorian ware, and 50s, 60s and 70s retro "stuff."

Perhaps the biggest sur-

94

prise, in a good way, to a first time visitor, is the abundance of furniture.

"We have an outstanding, very knowledgeable staff, well-trained in what we sell here in the mall," Denise adds.

Shoppers can only imagine what an undertaking it must have been to pack up and move their 200 dealers to the current location of 56,000 square feet.

The business also offers up an eatery, Colonnade Café, for customers who might want to take a break. After all, shopping and eating go hand-in-hand and a visit here lets you enjoy both. The eatery is located on the top floor.

SHOPPERS INFO ?

Address:
834 E. Broadway
Hours:
10 a.m. - 6 p.m., Monday - Saturday
12 noon - 6 p.m., Sunday
Phone:
502/333-6195
Area Attractions:
Kentucky Derby Museum, Louisville Slugger Museum, Muhammad Ali Museum, and much, much more.

Maker's Mark
LORETTA, KY

"I have recollections of many of the old bourbon barons," says Bill Samuels, Jr., President of Maker's Mark. "They were on their last leg when I was a young boy, but I knew them all."

It all comes together in the new Maker's Mark $2.5 million dollar visitors center/gift shop in Loretta, located in Marion County.

Located in a 19th century rickhouse, on the beautiful distillery grounds, the gift shop features a large assortment of Maker's Mark and bourbon-themed items. The shop's sleek, modern décor of copper and wood represents the distilleries move into the "modern era" of bourbon that began when Bill Samuels, Sr. created his special recipe found in every bottle of Maker's Mark today.

The present Maker's Mark distillery dates back to 1953, when Bill, Sr. purchased and refurbished the property that itself dates back to 1805 as a gristmill and distillery.

The picturesque grounds and unique buildings that surround the distillery make for a wonderful experience for visitors.

Guided tours of the property and distillation process are the highlight. However, some might argue that the professional sampling of the whiskey in the tasting lounge is the best part of all.

The center also features the recreated kitchen of Marge Samuels, Bill's mother. There are recipes of the wheat bread used in Maker's Mark, and even the frying pan she used to melt and dip the famous red wax seal used on all of the bottles. The study and library of what was their former home are filled with family memorabilia and art work including "talking photos."

"I think if my father were to come back today," says Samuels, "he would be most proud of the fact that the entire bourbon industry has uplifted. And it is now a showcase for the state of Kentucky."

SHOPPERS INFO

Address:
3350 Burks Spring Road

Hours:
Guided tours every hour on the half hour from 10:30 a.m. – 3:30 p.m., EST, Monday – Saturday, 1:30 p.m., 2:30 p.m., 3:30 p.m. during the months of March – December

Phone:
270/865-2099

Area Attractions:
Civil War History, area distilleries

Making Ends Meet
SHELBYVILLE, KY

When visitors first see the beautiful three-story house at 701 Washington Street in Shelbyville, little do they realize that inside is housed a fantastic fabric store.

Each of the businesses 12 rooms offers to customers an eye-opening experience. With an incredible selection of interior fabrics to include upholstery, cotton, silk, tapestry, linen, denim, suede, velvet, chenille, sheer and even outdoor fabrics. Custom one-of-a-kind furniture, pillows, table skirts, toppers and accent pieces abound throughout the store.

And all of these are at discount prices!

To add to the luster of Making Ends Meet, *Southern Living* magazine has listed the shop as one of the top fabric stores in the south.

Jeff and Leslie McCarthy opened the business in 1989, and the evolution of the inventory has been rewarding to the shoppers. The exquisite fabrics, trims, and home accessories allow both the casual shopper

and the professional designer to find exactly what they are looking for.

Jeff and Leslie take their services a step further with their in-house design staff. Almost any product can be custom made with those materials purchased here. They'll even refer customers to expert and talented seamstresses or upholsterers to complete a project.

A home, office, boat or RV can be outfitted from an interior standpoint from the literally thousands of fabrics and hundreds of trims this store offers.

It's easy to see why even "big city" customers come to this store to shop.

Some people might question how a person could get excited about a fabric store. This one shows you why.

"One of the things we really push is customer service when people come in our shop," says Leslie. "Our sales associates are very knowledgeable."

SHOPPERS INFO

Address:
701 Washington Street
Hours:
10 a.m. - 5 p.m., Monday - Saturday
Phone:
502/633-5427
Area Attractions:
Horses

Maple Hill Manor, Farm, Store and Studio
SPRINGFIELD, KY

Todd Allen and Tyler Horton operate a most unique shopping as well as educational experience in all of Kentucky.

They've turned their historic 1851 Maple Hill Manor into a topnotch bed and breakfast, but also an Alpaca and Llama farm with a shop full of merchandise.

The Springfield, Kentucky farm is the first of its kind dedicated to breeding Suris Alpacas and Llamas. Suri Alpacas represent only two percent of the total Alpaca population in the world, and their fleece is considered to be among the finest fibers in the world.

Alpaca-made garments are sold in their shop, called Manor Cottage Gifts.

It all began as something different in the way of a unique farm experi-

ence for guests at the B & B. Then it led to letting the general public in on it.

Alpaca-made items include hats, scarves, shawls, sweaters, Teddy Bears, pillows, blankets, socks, gloves, coats, jackets, rugs, slippers, capes, robes, yarn and throws. The shop also carries several Kentucky-made items.

Todd and Tyler don't plan on stopping here. They plan on expanding the farm store, adding an educational training center and fiber processing studio.

SHOPPERS INFO

Address:
2941 Perryville Road (US 150 East)
Hours:
12 noon – 4 p.m., Tuesday – Sunday
OR
by appointment
Phone:
1-800/886-7546
Area Attractions:
Lincoln Homestead State Park, Perryville Civil War Battlefield

The former 360,000 square foot Fisher Meat Packing Company has been turned into a mega shopping and art complex that is only going to get better with time.

Conceived in 2003, by the Clark family in Louisville, the "new" Mellwood Arts and Entertainment Center has become a maze of artist, studios, galleries, cafes and the so-called unusual retail shops.

This place is so big you may not realize there are as many individual businesses here as there are. Without question Mellwood is a work in progress, but anyone can see this should become something really special. That's why I felt like it deserved to be in this book. Just looking at the huge brick building and visualizing what it once was, and what it is evolving into is worth the trip.

Already there are quite a few first class shopping venues. And with all of the open-view art studios this is really going to be a fun place to visit.

The Center was originally created to be an economical place for artists to work and sell their creations directly to the public without waiting for acceptance from a gallery.

Presently there is a courtyard full of artists-owned shops that lead to other working artist studios. In some cases artist have the ability to "whip up a finished piece on the spot."

With the availability of meeting and special event rooms for weddings, fundraisers and corporate parties, it's no wonder this place is drawing a lot of attention throughout the Louisville area.

I was particularly drawn to three ground level shops. Patticakes

(formerly Elegance in Kentucky) sells novelty "Hat Box Patti Cakes." They are cakes baked to fit inside beautiful hat boxes. They are made in three different sizes and 52 different flavors. I can't wait to try the seasonal egg nog.

A few doors down is the Walnut Creek Rustic and Lodge Living Store. A most unusual place for sure. Believe me, you can't find this type of store on any corner. This store is packed with high end furniture and accessories for that special log house or cabin by the lake. Lamps, dishes, tables, rugs, beds, you name it and they've got it.

Across the way is Gallery Janjobe. This shop is owned by a group of artists, and as you would expect, it features a diverse collection of their works as well as others.

SHOPPERS INFO

Address:
1860 Mellwood Avenue
Hours:
Open seven days a week
Phone:
502/895-3650
Area Attraction:
Louisville

CENTRAL

Metzger's Country Store
SIMPSONVILLE, KY

his is about as unique as it gets. It's a sure bet you won't find many like it anywhere, even in Kentucky.

What started out as a little 600 square foot store selling mostly horse feed has turned into a "country store," that sells just about anything you need for taking care of your pets.

Brothers Charlie and Gary Metzger and their respective families operate a 7,000 square foot store with another 5,500 square foot of warehouse.

"We call it a country store and more," says Charlie.

There is an incredible inventory of pet food, 400 varieties in fact, horse feed and supplies, wild bird needs, gifts for the pet and pet owner, and when spring rolls around the most beautiful flowers.

Everything for the horse, rider, and even the trailer is sold here. Bird houses, feeders and more varieties of seed than you would believe.

Metzger's horse department offers English and Western tacks, barn equipment and supplements, as well as horse bedding.

Their mobile track truck can often be seen at Churchill Downs and Keeneland Race Course. It is fully stocked with everything that trainers, jockeys and exercise riders need, and further emphasizes that Metzger's caters to the professionals as well as amateurs.

Humans haven't been left out either. They carry Carhart winter gear, riding wear, and Montana Silversmith jewelry and statues, equestrian jewelry and a hugh gift department.

Metzger's is one of those places that you've got to visit. Even if you don't purchase something, it's a neat place to browse.

It's easy to see and, yes, believe the stores motto? "Animals make people happy...we make animals happy."

SHOPPERS INFO ?

Address:
6791 Shelbyville Road
Hours:
9 a.m. - 6:30 p.m., Monday – Saturday
12 noon – 5 p.m., Sunday
Phone:
502/722-8850
Area Attractions:
Shelby County Horse Farms, Louisville

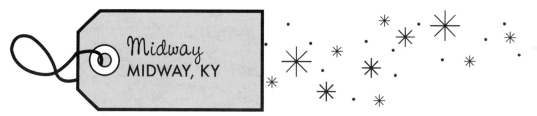

Midway
MIDWAY, KY

Midway lays claim to be Kentucky's first railroad town. Whether it is or isn't makes little difference. Tracks do indeed run right down the middle of town with shops and restaurants on either side. I have to say with such prominence of train tracks, it looks like a railroad town to me, and quite possibly the first.

This little town in Woodford County is one of the most charming in all of Kentucky. Named because it is "midway" between Frankfort and Lexington, and "midway" between Georgetown and Versailles, its Railroad Street is lined with antique shops, book stores and cafes. Several B & B's and outstanding restaurants are handy, thus making this a destination trip for those wanting to overnight.

Nearby scenic horse farms make for enjoyable excursions as does strolling around town, taking in some or all of the 176 buildings listed in the National Register of Historic Places.

The town is also home to Midway College, an independent liberal arts school for women. Wiesenberger Mill, a sixth generation business is the oldest continuously operating mill in Kentucky, and Zeralda Cole James, the mother of legendary outlaws Jesse and Frank James, was born in the Block Horse Inn located at

the intersection of U.S. 62 and Old Frankfort Pike. And who would have ever guessed that the Porterhouse steak originated in the old Porter House still standing on Winter Street.

SHOPPERS INFO ?

Address:
Just off I-64, exit 65
Hours:
Stores and shop hours vary, but generally open 10 a.m. – 5 p.m.
Phone:
City of Midway – 859/846-4413
Area Attractions:
Horse Farms, Scenic Byways

Muth's Candies
LOUISVILLE, KY

Since 1921 Muth's has been making and selling candy in Louisville. Well, actually that's not completely true. Because now they actually sell it all over the world.

"We ship our candy everywhere," says owner Martha Vories. "You just can't believe the customers we've had in here over the years and many continue to order it all the time."

Martha is a fourth generation owner and operator of Muth's, and along with her husband Stephen, they continue to turn out a world-class candy. It is a fact, only the highest quality of ingredients is used here. It shows up in every bite.

When Rudy Muth returned to Louisville following World War I he followed his dream of opening up a candy shop. It's important to note that there were already several in the city. In fact there were already a few in Rudy's East Market neighborhood. He knew if he was going to make it his candy had to be great!

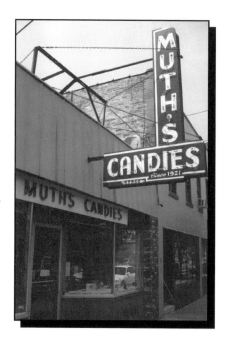

It was, and still is.

Rudy, and his wife Isabell, built the business with family and lots of friends. It endured to become Louisville's oldest and finest candy shop.

Muth's is a success story of craftsmanship being delicately handed down from one generation to another. To the family, candy making is an art form. The same recipes are still used. Some specialized in stirring the copper

kettle, others were responsible for hand-dipping the centers in rich chocolate, while others wrapped and packaged the treats for sale to eager customers.

Today when you walk in the front door, what you see is much the way it looked in 1921. The old glass cases allow customers to have a good look at the finished chocolates.

One of the "house favorites" is modjeska, a precise combination of a soft marshmallow covered with a light caramel covering.

The bourbon balls are made with 100 proof Kentucky's finest and then dipped in a rich semi-sweet chocolate. And then there are the classic cherries that feature a plump cherry floating in a rich cream inside a delicious chocolate shell.

The selections go on and on. Cinnamon creams, peanut butter cream, pineapple cream, chocolate fudge, chocolate drops, lemon jelly...the list just doesn't stop.

This is absolutely an "I have to go there" place. Another absolute is you will not leave without a sack full of candy.

SHOPPERS INFO ?

Address:
360 E. Market Street
Hours:
8:30 a.m. - 4 p.m., Tuesday - Friday
10 a.m. - 4 p.m., Saturday
Closed Sunday & Monday
Special Holiday Hours - Call in advance
Phone:
502/585-2952
Area Attractions:
Joe Ley Antiques, Museums, Shops

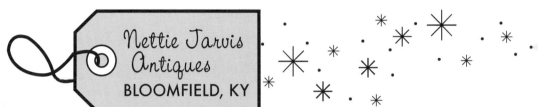

Nettie Jarvis Antiques
BLOOMFIELD, KY

When I visited Bloomfield a few years ago, it had been over 40 years since my last trip there. I had no reason to return. My high school basketball team had lost a game there, and our yellow bus left immediately afterwards, under the cover of darkness.

Good riddance.

But that was then, and this is now, and I love going back to Bloomfield.

A few years ago Linda Bruckheimer and her husband Jerry, bought a farm near Bloomfield and renovated and restored an 1820 Greek-revival house on the property. With her younger years spent in Louisville, she decided to follow her dream, step out of the "LA fast lane," and return to her roots.

I can tell you first hand Kentucky, and Bloomfield in particular, is better for it.

Not long ago Linda bought and restored an old 1899 building in the small town with just over 1,000 population. Then she bought another, and soon after another, until she now owns five.

With a fine eye to detail and a simplistic vision for the future, she has helped to make Bloomfield not only a fun place, but a must place to visit.

One of the buildings is the Olde Bloomfield Meeting Hall that is now a family recreation facility where children and their parents can bowl, skate, shoot pool and play pinball.

Across the street is

Nettie Jarvis Antiques, named after Linda's great grandmother. It's a destination shop that has gained a reputation for high quality merchandise throughout Kentucky and the South. It is considered Bloomfield's main attraction, and rightfully so.

The historic two-story, 5,000 square foot building has been carefully restored and houses an inventory of high-end 18th and 19th century Kentucky and American furniture, coin silver, primitives and quilts.

SHOPPERS INFO

Address:
111 Taylorsville Road
Hours:
10 a.m. - 6 p.m., Tuesday - Saturday
Closed Sunday and Monday
Open by appointment
Phone:
502/252-9555
Area Attractions:
Taylorsville Lake, Distilleries, Bardstown

Poor Richards Books & Completely Kentucky
FRANKFORT, KY

$\mathcal{W}$hat a special shopping treat this turned out to be. These are actually two separate businesses located side-by-side with a cut-through. Customers get to enjoy both shops regardless of which door they enter.

The two shops are located across the street from Kentucky's historic Old Capital building in downtown Frankfort.

Poor Richard's Books is one of those wonderful independent bookstores that upon entering, you might wonder what took you so long to visit this place.

Thousands of books line the walls, are stacked on tables, and showcased on shelves.

Richard and Lizz Taylor oversee the store, and even though the name is catchy, there's nothing poor about this store.

Poor Richard's specializes in Kentucky titles, but believe me they have much more. Customers usually enjoy the sounds of Kentucky music, and, when inclined to do so, can savor one of their tempting scones and a hot or iced latte.

"Customers are sure to find what they need to complete their Kentucky collection," offers Lizz Taylor.

Richard, her husband, is a former Poet Laureate of Kentucky.

Completely Kentucky

The Kentucky theme continues full speed ahead when you walk into Completely Kentucky. This carefully restored 150-year-old building offers works from over 450 of Kentucky's best artisans.

"We buy directly from the artists," says owner Ann Wingrove. "So we know each personally."

Completely Kentucky has one of the largest selections of Kentucky arts and crafts and Kentucky gourmet foods anywhere.

"Every item in our store is made by one of Kentucky's finest cooks, artisans or craftspersons," adds Ann. "From traditional to contemporary, functional to decorative, fine art to funny, you can find it here."

SHOPPERS INFO

Poor Richards
Address:
233 West Broadway
Hours:
9:30 a.m. - 8 p.m., Monday - Friday
9:30 a.m. - 5 p.m., Saturday
12:30 p.m. - 5 p.m., Sunday
Phone:
502/223-8018

Completely Kentucky
Address:
235 West Broadway
Hours:
9 a.m. - 5 p.m., Monday - Saturday
12:30 p.m. - 5 p.m., Sunday
Phone:
1/800-457-1990
Area Attractions:
State Capital

RidgeMont Furniture Galleries
SHEPHERDSVILLE, KY

a trip to RidgeMont is a shopping experience.

I can remember for years hearing about this big, old furniture store in Shepherdsville that had been there for a long time. Its name was Henderson Hardy Furniture, and it had a good reputation for quality furniture at a low price.

The old turn-of-the-century store is still there, but back in 1997 two former Hardy employees bought the business, and after blending their two names, they now have RidgeMont Furniture Galleries.

Aileen Wooldridge and Ronnie Montgomery have one of the most fascinating stores of its kind in the state. The building is huge, and I can tell you first hand it's easy to get lost in these 50,000 square feet of showrooms. Shoppers will weave to the left, then to the right, up a little here, and down and around there, forgetting where you started. All the while admiring the beautiful vignettes of bedrooms, dining rooms, living rooms, office furniture complete with carefully thought out accessories. At any given time there are 100 sofas and 25 bedrooms displayed for customers to consider.

"We carry furniture from over 100 companies, such as Sherrill, King Hickory, Lane, Sumter, Cochrane, Century, Hickory White, Hooker, Stanley, and Magnessum, which features the Biltmore Collection," Aileen Wooldridge proudly offers.

This is a serious store, complete with knowledgeable sales people who know fabrics, carpets, lamps and direction. They even have a floral designer on staff. Any of these folks can point you in the right direction, and help you get back if needed.

A first-Saturday-in-November Christmas Open House has become a local event that draws from the surrounding area.

SHOPPERS INFO ?

Address:
416 S. Buckman Street
I-65, exit 117

Hours:
10 a.m. – 8 p.m., Monday & Thursday
10 a.m. – 5 p.m., Tuesday, Wednesday, Friday & Saturday
Closed Sunday

Phone:
502/955-1654

Area Attractions:
Hawks View Gallery, Bernheim Forest, Jim Beam Distillery

Ruth Hunt Candies
MT. STERLING, KY

Ruth Tharpe Hunt was hosting her bridge club. As was often done in 1920, she served up some sweets she had prepared in her kitchen in Mt. Sterling.

Not long after, with encouragement from friends, in 1921 she started a small candy business. She had turned a hobby into a business, and today Ruth Hunt Candies ships its chocolates all over the world.

Among the 70 varieties of candies at Ruth Hunt's are cream candy, bourbon balls, caramels, assorted soft creams and sugar free chocolate. If this shop is known for one thing, it is the "Blue Monday". It's a pulled cream candy center covered in a dark chocolate. This bar was developed as the result of a traveling minister, who over 60 years ago, would stop by and tell Ruth he "needed a little sweet to cure his blue Monday."

Toby Moore, the manager at Ruth Hunt Candies has been there for over 20 years. He proudly points out that only the finest qualities of ingredients are used in making all of the store's products.

"We use real whipping cream, dairy butter and fresh roasted nuts," he says. "And we do it all with chocolate that has no additives."

The huge old marble slabs allow for cinnamon suckers to be formed, while caramels are stirred in giant copper kettles.

All of this and much more can be seen on the free tours offered at Ruth Hunt. The tour begins with a short video detailing the history of candy and the different processes. From there you are led to the "back room" production area.

In 1993, Ruth Hunt Candies became the "official candy maker" of Churchill Downs and the Kentucky Derby. Boxes and tins can be purchased with Derby scenes reproduced from an oil painting by noted Kentucky artist Joyce Garner.

Ruth Hunt Candies are often sold in major gift shops throughout the state, but there's nothing like visiting the site where it is actually made.

Of course, during the almost ninety years of producing candy, lots of people, some not so famous and some famous, have ordered candy from here. One year a 60-pound order went to the White House. Lady Byrd Johnson purchased it for the Christmas season in Washington. I have a feeling some it found its way to Texas.

SHOPPERS INFO ?

Address:
550 N. Maysville Road
I-64, exit 110
Hours:
9 a.m. – 5:30 p.m., Monday – Saturday
1 p.m. – 5:30 p.m., Sunday
Phone:
800/927-0302
Area Attractions:
Old Silo Golf Course

*L*ocated just a stones throw from Harrodsburg, Shaker Village is a unique place to visit even if it didn't offer a most unusual place to shop.

Shaker Village of Pleasant Hill is the largest historic community of its kind in America, and its 2,800 acres of farmland operate just as it did in the 19th century. Visitors can see trades being taught such as furniture making and basket weaving, and believe it or not, an instructional class is offered on how to work a team of harnessed horses in the field. Although this may not be to your liking, it's still nice to know there is someplace in the United States that keeps alive the values of hardworking people in days gone by.

What might be to your liking is the wonderful dining (reservations preferred) and shopping experience offered here at Shaker Village.

The Carpenter's Shop Craft Store is the village's main craft store and gift shop. Plan on spending a little time here because the shop offers an extensive selection of fine handmade items not found anywhere else. It fea-

tures Shaker reproduction furniture, painstakingly reproduced or adapted from original museum collection pieces. Handmade brooms and an assortment of oval boxes in different sizes are staples of the shop. Highly skilled artisans craft many of the items for sale using the identical techniques that have made "Shaker-crafted" synonymous with quality throughout the 19th century and today.

The Post Office Craft Store is the smaller of the two shops at Shaker Village. It offers up selective Kentucky foods, kitchen accessories, hand-dipped candles and candleholders.

The ambiance of Shaker Village at Pleasant Hill is a family-fun stop. Costumed interpreters make for an interesting story about the Shakers of the past. Also, self-guided walking tours are very popular and include 14 of the village's 34 restored buildings.

Fifteen of these buildings serve as lodging facilities totaling 81 rooms for guests.

SHOPPERS INFO ?

Address:
3501 Lexington Road
Hours:
Winter: 10 a.m. – 4:30 p.m., tours
10 a.m. – 5 p.m., craft store
Summer: 9 a.m. – 5 p.m., tours
9:30 a.m. – 5:30 p.m., craft store
Open every day except Christmas Eve & Christmas Day
Phone:
859/734-5411 or 800/734-5611
Area Attractions:
Old Fort Harrod State Park, Beaumont Inn

Shannon Lamps
LEXINGTON, KY

Shannon Lamp Service is definitely a one-of-a-kind. Peering into the back room, just beyond the showroom, is like looking into the back lot of a Hollywood movie set. Lamps, lamp parts, shades, fabrics and machinery are everywhere. All go into making this shop a Lexington institution.

Begun in 1956 by Coleman Shannon, it has survived the onslaught of cheap lamps and even cheaper mass-produced shades.

Today Coleman's son, David and his wife, Amy, pretty much run the daily operation, but don't underestimate the elder Shannon's role in the business. Not only does he do lamps, but also stained glass and chair caning.

If you can think it up, there's a good chance they can make a lamp. Everything made at Shannon's is done so one at a time. You don't stay in business this long without doing something right.

Visitors can't help but notice the huge "leg lamp" in the showroom. This is the lamp made famous in the television movie classic, *A Christ-*

mas Story. And speaking of movies, a buyer for Steven Spielberg came into Shannon's and bought up nine lamps for the *Dreamer* movie set. One happened to be a custom-made horse-themed lamp with a spinning shade.

"It's amazing how many people saw it and wanted it," David Shannon said.

One customer said she likes the fact that they do things here one-at-a-time, and offer good hard-to-find customer service.

"We can customize any lamp or replace any shade," David says. "Just bring it in."

Shannon Lamps is a business that defines what small family business is all about.

The easiest way to get to Shannon's is to get on New Circle Road, go to Limestone, and travel three blocks.

SHOPPERS INFO ?

Address:
1210 Limestone
Hours:
9 a.m. – 5 p.m., Monday – Friday
9 a.m. – 3 p.m., Saturday
Phone:
859/255-5285
Area Attractions:
Horse Farm Tours, University of Kentucky

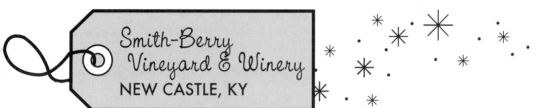

Smith-Berry Vineyard & Winery
NEW CASTLE, KY

When Mary and Chuck Smith decided several years ago to replace their tobacco with grapes on their Henry County farm, a whole lot of people were better for it. Especially those of us who enjoy a glass of wine every now and then.

Smith-Berry Vineyard and Winery is a delightful result of a Kentucky farming family deciding to change direction.

"Our research revealed that the soil and weather here was close to what was happening in the wine growing regions of France," offered Chuck.

And what was even better was they learned that an acre of grapes would pay as much, if not more, than an acre of tobacco.

The Smiths are still farmers, and proud of it. They raise organic beef cattle, sheep, hay crops and organic vegetables for their own use as well as the special events that take place at their winery.

Their 180-acre farm has five of those acres devoted to growing grapes of three different varieties.

"We chose Chambourcin and Norton, for their qualities as a red wine, and Vidal Blanc that produces an off-dry to sweet white wine," Mary Berry-Smith explains.

The Smiths' are quick to give credit to daughters Katie, Virginia and Tonya for the success of the winery.

The big barn on the property serves as the gallery and winery, and here visitors can purchase an as-

sortment of wines to include dry reds, dry whites, sweet wines, and their reserve and specialty wines.

Of course a visit here would not be complete unless you sampled the product at Smith-Berry. A tasting room, surrounded by other neat things for sale makes this a fun place to shop.

Picnic items, cheeses, jams, jellies, salsas, are all things that could, and often do, accompany a nice glass of wine.

Smith-Berry Vineyard and Winery offers seasonal concerts and special events.

SHOPPERS INFO

Address:
855 Drennon Road
Hours:
10 a.m. – 6 p.m., Tuesday – Saturday
Phone:
502/845-7091
Area Attractions:
Chat n Nibble Restaurant, Our Best Restaurant

The Plaid Rabbit
MT. STERLING, KY

Mt. Sterling is a fun place to visit. It's one of those charming small towns where you can park your car downtown on a nice day and stroll around the square just enjoying the historic architecture and friendly people.

By all means you've got to visit The Plaid Rabbit. It's one of those wonderful little gift shops that are so much fun to discover in a small town. It may be in a small town, but the store sells big city merchandise.

Roberta Gilbert, and her daughter Beverly, opened The Plaid Rabbit back in 1998.

"She was still in college at the time," Roberta says referring to her daughter. "She was studying marketing and we both thought it was the thing to do."

The two, along with Roberta's mother, oversee the store, and over the years have built up a clientele from, not just Mt. Sterling, but the surrounding area.

"We are not pushy salespeople," Roberta adds. "We just let people come in and look around on their own and answer any questions."

Bridal registries are a big part of this shops activity. This is a sure sign that a shop has high end merchandise.

Lots of Kentucky-made products and books line the stores shelves.

"We are adding more Kentucky gourmet items all the time," says Roberta.

A real surprise for visitors in the shop for the first time is the merchandise geared toward college fraternity and sororities.

"We have really made a name for ourselves," she offers, as she points to the Greek section. "Lots of students and their families come in from schools in the area, but it's neat to have items shipped to Western Kentucky University, University of Florida, Wake Forest and University of South Florida, just to name a few."

The shop also has an in-house artist that can personalize certain items.

At The Plaid Rabbit you can expect to see lots of neat kitchen accessories, hand bags, bar related items, sterling silver jewelry, baby gifts, dinnerware, home décor, stationary and monogrammed jewelry.

SHOPPERS INFO

Address:
39 S. Maysville Street
Hours:
10 a.m. - 5 p.m., Monday - Friday
10 a.m. - 4 p.m., Saturday
Phone:
859/498-2300
Area Attractions:
Historic Downtown, Old Silo Golf Course

a candy store only a few feet from a statue of Abraham Lincoln and the Lincoln Museum in downtown Hodgenville only adds to the enjoyment of celebrating the Lincoln Bicentennial.

If you haven't been to Hodgenville lately, you may not recognize it. The downtown's "square area" has undergone an extensive renovation in anticipation of the thousands of visitors who will flock to this small Larue County town that is the birthplace of Abraham Lincoln, the nation's sixteenth president.

Believe me, however, you don't have to wait for any celebration to visit The Sweet Shoppe.

It is a gourmet fudge shop with over 40 varieties of rich, creamy homemade fudge.

Owners, Patrick and Paula Durham, use double boiler kettles to prepare their sweets, and one of the things you've got to admire about them

is their willingness to try new flavors.

"We are constantly experimenting with new flavors," offers Patrick. "We even welcome any suggestions for new flavors. We'll try them."

One of the fun things to do when you visit a place like The Sweet Shoppe is to sample a taste of some of the fudge you haven't tried before.

How about a bite of creamsicle, or cookies and cream, or French vanilla, or raspberry chocolate swirl, or snickers or butterfinger, or butter brickle crunch? Wait a minute! Why not try them all!

Don't you like the signs posted in shops like this that tell you they "will ship." Who wants to ship when you can take this with you? The shipping thing, however, is when you get home and decide you have to have some more. Thank goodness they ship!

The Durham's say peanut butter is at the top of the best seller list. But, also is their Kentucky bourbon, rich smooth chocolate fudge infused with Kentucky's finest and liberally accented with pecans and walnuts. You also will lick your lips when you bite into the tiger fudge. It is vanilla fudge swirled with melted peanut butter and topped with a drizzle of chocolate fudge. "It's a local favorite," says Patrick.

I know a few visitors who will like it, too!

SHOPPERS INFO

Address:
100 South Lincoln Boulevard
Hours:
11 a.m. – 6 p.m., Monday – Saturday
Closed Sunday
Phone:
270/358-0424
Area Attractions:
Lincoln's Birthplace, Lincoln Museum, Lincoln's Boyhood Home

CENTRAL

U.S. Cavalry Store
RADCLIFF, KY

It's a guarantee there's not another store like this in the book.

U.S. Cavalry got started back in the early 70s when owner Randy Acton began selling permanent press Army fatigues to soldiers out of the back of a truck he set up just outside of the gate at Fort Knox. Up until then it was starch and a hot iron. Because the military supply chain at the time had not yet made them available, they were quite popular.

From the truck to a warehouse to a retail store, U.S. Cavalry grew, specializing in military, police and outdoor camping equipment and products. It is said that at one time this store even sold to foreign governments for their armies.

This is a type of store that most people don't even know exists, mainly because the general public doesn't have a need for most of their products, at least on a regular basis. You can be sure, however, that the nation's security and public protection agencies probably know all about it. It is often referred to as a one-stop cop shop.

U.S. Cavalry is a serious store when it comes to clothing, gloves, eyewear, footwear, rappelling, weapons, body armor, packs, field equipment, medical equipment, knives, tools and lights.

This store is a very high volume mail order facility that sits just off of 31-W in Radcliff, near Fort Knox. A 65,000 square foot storage-warehouse allows orders and stock to be delivered at a fairly rapid pace.

This unique operation is a must visit even if you only want to look around.

SHOPPERS INFO

Address:
2855 Centennial Avenue
Hours:
9 a.m. – 7 p.m., Monday – Saturday
9 a.m. – 5 p.m., Sunday
Phone:
800/777-7172 or 270/351-7000
Area Attractions:
Gold Vault at Ft. Knox, Coca-Cola Museum

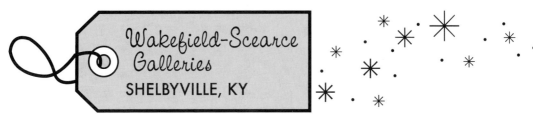

Wakefield-Scearce Galleries
SHELBYVILLE, KY

Wakefield-Scearce Galleries is quite a place, to say the least. Located in what is called Science Hill, a former school for young ladies that began in 1825, this incredible shop features over 32,000 square feet of showrooms of English Georgian antiques.

First opened in 1947 by Mark Wakefield and Mark Scearce, they immediately began importing merchandise from the British Isles. Since then, the gallery has maintained an impressive inventory of antique furniture, silver, paintings and accessories showcased throughout its four levels.

With antiques of British origin strategically placed, the shop takes on a museum-like appearance, as visitors talk quietly as they traverse from room to room.

Vivid colors, heavily-draped windows, well-appointed dining room table settings, candelabras, over-stuffed chairs, thick framed paintings, delicate porcelain and china, fancy lamps, and silver, like you've never seen before, all make this one of the largest single collections in the country.

Over the years important and famous people have visited here, but owner Pat Burnett is quick to say that everyone from all walks of life is welcome at Wakefield-Scearce Galleries.

Yes, it's true the store does, indeed have an uppity feel, but at the same time it's comforting in that you are able to relive some of the past while browsing these fabulous antiques.

Burnett is the son-in-law of co-founder Mark Scearce.

"I started working here in 1978 and became president upon Mr. Scearce's passing," he says.

Probably the one thing this shop is best known for is their sterling silver julep cups. President George Bush has used them as gifts to foreign dignitaries when visiting the United States.

Science Hill Restaurant and several other shops are also located under the same roof.

SHOPPERS INFO ?

Address:
525 Washington Street
Hours:
9 a.m. – 5 p.m., Monday – Saturday
Closed Sunday
Phone:
502/633-4382
Area Attractions:
Horse Farms and Tours

Willcutt Guitar Shoppe
LEXINGTON, KY

$\mathcal{H}$ow many times have we judged a business by the façade of the building? I've done it, but not anymore. I decided sometime ago not to pass judgment until I got inside.

I urge you not to pre-judge this unassuming; two-story building that once was a grocery store. Today, the white building, with the big "W" on the front is a world class guitar store, and owner Bob Willcutt has built the business into one of the strongest independent music stores in the country.

"We can repeatedly claim to be the number one dealer in the world for many high end brands," offers Bob.

And when he refers to high end, he's talking about PRS Guitars, Hamer Guitars, Dr. Z Amps, Carr Amps, Breedlove Guitars, Nik Huber guitars, and Bad Cat Amps.

Willcutt's is also one of the country's top dealers in Gibson, Fender and Taylor.

Bob is big into the WOW factor. And when you walk into his store if you don't say it, you at least think it. WOW!

Guitars in every color and style look like pieces of art clinging to every wall and available space.

"I have found a way to mix my love of art and passion for guitars with our special run of 'art guitars' from PRS, Gibson and Taylor," added Bob. "These are the kind of items that not only can be played, but can be hung on a wall to WOW anyone who sees them."

Bob came to Lexington as a student at the University of Kentucky. With a background of high

school bands, he soon found himself doing guitar repairs for friends. One thing led to another, and he began working part time for a local music store as a repair man.

Anyone who stops in Willcutt Guitar Shoppe will usually find Bob doing what he enjoys most: back in the shop building a guitar or tweaking a new one before sending it out to its new owner.

Willcutt's has customers from all 50 states, many from the internet.

"Many customers who purchased items through the web have made pilgrimages to see our store in person and meet the people with whom they have developed a phone rapport," Bob says.

This store sells the finest instruments in the market today!

SHOPPERS INFO ?

Address:
419 Rosemont Garden
Hours:
11 a.m. - 7 p.m., Monday - Friday
11 a.m. - 5 p.m., Saturday
Phone:
859/276-2713
Area Attractions:
Horse Farms

BARBARA STEWART INTERIORS	BOWLING GREEN, KY
DENNISON'S ROADSIDE MARKET	UNO, KY
DETWEILER'S COUNTRY STORE	CUB RUN, KY
DINOSAUR WORLD GIFT SHOP	CAVE CITY, KY
JUNEBUGS	GLASGOW, KY
K & H DEPARTMENT STORE	HORSE CAVE, KY
KENTUCKY STATE PARK GIFT SHOPS	STATEWIDE (PAGE 34)
KNOT-HEAD	SOMERSET, KY
MAGNOLIA ALLEY	CAMPBELLSVILLE, KY
MOORE'S SHOE STORE	CAMPBELLSVILLE, KY
PARADISE POINT	SCOTTSVILLE, KY
PAUL'S DISCOUNT	SOMERSET, KY
PISTOLS N' PETTICOATS	FRANKLIN, KY
RILEY'S BAKERY	BOWLING GREEN, KY
SOUTHERN OUTDOOR FURNITURE	AUBURN, KY
STEVE'S SPORTS CARDS	BOWLING GREEN, KY
THE KLASSIC SHOP	ALBANY, KY
V & R ENTERPRISES	BROWNSVILLE, KY
WILD BIRD AND NATURE STORE	BOWLING GREEN, KY

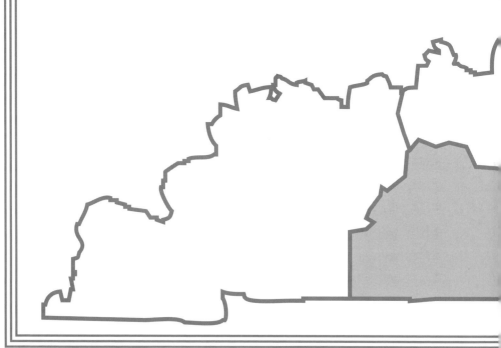

SOUTH CENTRAL
REGION

Barbara Stewart Interiors
BOWLING GREEN, KY

There are so many things to like about this shop that I don't know where to begin. Okay, let's start with the location.

Located in Bowling Green's beautiful historic downtown on Fountain Square, Barbara Stewart Interiors has been a family-run business since 1952. In 1979, Barbara moved to the present location at 444 Main.

The shop is a combination of two former stores that date back to the turn of the century, and the exposed interior brick walls, combined with hardwood floors, all add to the elegance of a shopping experience.

Susan Hoechner, Barbara's daughter, runs this fantastic gift shop now. The shop, at first blush, takes on the appearance of a museum, but after a few steps inside, visitors quickly realize this is a "shopper-friendly" establishment.

"We believe that your home should reflect your personal style," offers Susan. "And for over 55 years we have been helping our customers create unique, classic and ageless interiors through custom picture framing, fine home furnishings, decorative accessories and interior design services."

Just about everything sold in this beautiful shop can stand the test of time in a home. From its jewelry, dinnerware, gourmet foods, stationary and floral arrangements, to antiques, beautiful reproductions, wallcoverings, mirrors and area rugs, to linens, chandeliers, lamps and draperies, this is a store that can hold its own with any store of its type in Kentucky.

"Our furnishings include some of the finest reproductions on the market today as well as antiques mixed in," says Susan.

With an education in interior design, Susan has over 30 years of experience in residential and commercial furnishings.

One of the nice things about Barbara Stewart Interiors is that the staff allows you to browse at your leisure, always ready to help when asked.

The shop has its own custom frame department for prints, original art (they sell!), and mirrors.

Oh, by the way, don't be surprised when upon entering the shop, you're greeted by Lizzie, a black tea-cup puddle, or Roxie, a miniature schnauzer. There's no charge for a friendly lick, nor is there for the complimentary gift wrapping.

SOUTH CENTRAL

SHOPPERS INFO

Address:
444 E. Main Street
Hours:
10 a.m. – 5:30 p.m., Monday – Friday
10 a.m. – 4 p.m., Saturday
Phone:
270/782-1747
Area Attractions:
National Corvette Museum, Historic Downtown, Historic Depot Museum, Kentucky Museum, Lost River Cave, Beech Bend Park

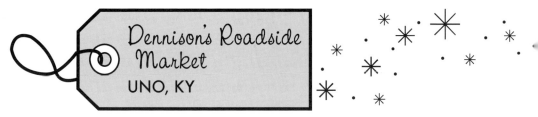

Dennison's Roadside Market
UNO, KY

There's no way you can drive by Dennison's Roadside Market between April 1 and November 15 without stopping. Located on 31-E between Glasgow and Uno, it is an oasis in the middle of what seems like nowhere. It is so inviting, and believe me it does not disappoint.

"We started out just selling tomatoes and pretty soon people wanted us to sell more," says Kathy Dennison, who along with husband Paul owns the business. "Before long we were growing green beans, corn, squash, zucchini, peppers, okra, cantaloupe, watermelons and pumpkins."

Not long after, the two decided to add on to an existing tobacco barn, and make an actual marketplace out of it. From there they enclosed the area, added air conditioning, coolers and a front porch they would encourage customers to sit awhile and possibly enjoy one of those small bottle Cokes.

At Dennison's it just kept getting better. Three greenhouses were built, and bedding plants, jalapenos, cabbage, cucumbers, blackberries,

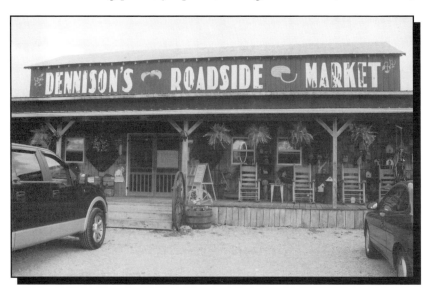

strawberries, blueberries, and raspberries were added to the inventory.

"We also grow cornshucks for fall decorations," says Kathy. "And inside we sell locally made jams and jellies from the Amish. We also carry handmade baskets, relishes, sorghums, honey, candles and lye soap."

As if what they have is not enough, Dennison's offers hay rides to school groups in October.

"They enjoy all of the pumpkins and farm animals we have," Kathy adds. "Cows, goats, sheep, pot belly pigs, rabbits, emus, pigeons, chickens, and a fish pond let them enjoy an atmosphere which some children never get to experience."

Visitors from as far away as Australia, Alaska, South Africa, Ireland, Norway and Finland have shopped at Dennison's Roadside Market.

SHOPPERS INFO

Address:
5824 S. Jackson Hwy. (31-E)
Hours:
8 a.m. – 6 p.m., Monday – Saturday
12 p.m. – 6 p.m., Sunday
Phone:
270/786-1663
Area Attractions:
Barren River Lake

Detweiler's Country Store
CUB RUN, KY

*C*ub Run is truly one of those communities off-the-beaten-path. But now there are a couple of good reasons to search out this town.

A couple of years ago Cub Run Cave was "reopened" to the public after being closed for well over a half-century. It is a beautiful show cave that makes for a delightful family outing away from the hustle and bustle.

Also away from the hustle and bustle and also in Cub Run is a "must visit."

Detweiler's Country Store, owned and operated by Dan and Ruth Detweiler, who moved to Kentucky from Ohio in 1997. As members of the Old Order Amish faith, they were in search for a slower pace of life. They soon found themselves the owners of a hardware and variety store then known as Farmwald's. They changed the name to Detweiler's, and before they knew it their little store began to grow.

Their business now consists of two buildings: one that is the country store, and the other that sells hardware and feed supplies.

From shelves of old-fashioned candies, to bulk food supplies, to Amish clothing and homemade baskets, it's a practical store that sells practical merchandise.

Its large selection of jigsaw puzzles is very popular with the customers, as are the singing clocks that sell so quickly that Ruth and Dan often don't get a chance to listen to their beautiful sounds.

Many of the locals are regulars when it comes to the store's homemade sandwiches, jams and jellies.

In the hardware portion of the store, merchandise consisting of plumbing, hardware, landscaping and feed is stacked from the floor to ceiling. Hanging from the massive beams are antique tools, tricycles and scooters.

Out back, a waterwheel delivers water into a pond filled with ducks and fish. Nearby, the Detweiler's have some miniature donkeys that are fun to see.

SHOPPERS INFO

Address:
12825 Priceville Road (Hwy. 728)
From Munfordville, Hwy. 88W to Cub Run, 10 miles turn right on 728
Hours:
8 a.m. – 5 p.m., Monday – Friday
8 a.m. – 4 p.m., Saturday
Closed Sunday
Phone:
270/524-7967
Area Attractions:
Cub Run Cave

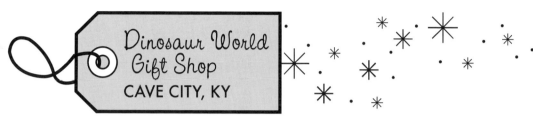

*a*ttractions and museum gift shops are about as rare in this book as what this one sells in its shop.

It's a guarantee there's not another one like this in Kentucky. It's all about the Dinosaur.

You don't have to pay an admission price to enter the 5,000-square-foot gift shop. However, you just might decide to do the whole tour once there.

What helps to make this shop unusual is there are actually two shops in one, one section for the kids and the other for grown-ups.

From glowing Dinosaurs to roaring Godzilla's, to children's apparel, this makes for really good gifts for all occasions.

The shop's Marquee collections are actual authentic dinosaur eggs, some priced at $6,000, dinosaur teeth, and claws of museum quality. And they are for sale to those serious collectors out there.

Almost everywhere you look there's dinosaur "stuff." T-Rex heads are mounted on the walls, as well as various sizes and shapes of dinosaur casts.

Anyone who has ever wanted to own an original fossil can now have that opportunity. Amethyst, amber, agate and an assortment of other

rocks have been turned into everything from jewelry to flatware and offered for sale.

The gift shop is proud of the educational literature it offers as well as an impressive array of books ranging from children's books to fictional literature to encyclopedias of fossils. Learning toys such as a variety of dinosaur models, miniature fossil digs, and interactive play sets are just a few of the reasons this is a great place to shop and visit with the kids in mind.

Dinosaur World is definitely one of those touristy things to do. But it's most certainly one of those places to keep in mind when wanting to buy that special person something totally different. You know, the person who has everything.

SHOPPERS INFO

Address:
711 Mammoth Cave Road
Exit 68 on I-65
Hours:
8:30 a.m. – 6 p.m., daily
Phone:
270/773-4345
Area Attractions:
Mammoth Cave, Kentucky Down Under, Diamond Caverns, Gun Town Mountain

Junebugs
GLASGOW, KY

It's what every store needs, especially one that caters to mothers who take their children with them when they go shopping: a designated play area where children can safely play while mom or dad shops.

Robin Garmon and Brandi Young own and operate Junebugs, an upscale children's boutique on the square in downtown Glasgow.

Robin and Brandi decided to open the shop because they felt a need for a one-of-a-kind place for children's clothing and gifts. No longer do the locals have to leave town to find that special item for the younger group.

"We try to not only offer great products," says Brandi. "But also a unique atmosphere and outstanding customer service."

Junebugs sees itself as the complete shop for children. From newborns through toddlers, it's all here. Diaper caddies, baby jewelry, hair bows, and you've got to see their custom-made "diaper cakes."

The shop carries clothing for both boys and girls with sizes ranging from 0 to 5T. Among the brands are Max n' Maddie, Hartstrings, Rosie Posie, Rosalina, Baby Togs and Lil Jellybeans.

It's also nice to see quality children's bedroom furniture that also includes an assortment of little wicker rockers. There's a real probability that if you take a toddler with you and he or she "tries the rocker out," you'll be taking one home with you. And I'm not talking about the toddler either!

Junebugs offers a custom embroidery service that allows most items in stock to have a personal touch.

SHOPPERS INFO ?

Address:
134 East Public Square
Hours:
9 a.m. - 5 p.m., Monday - Friday
10 a.m. - 4 p.m., Saturday
Phone:
270/834-1193
Area Attractions:
Barren River Lake

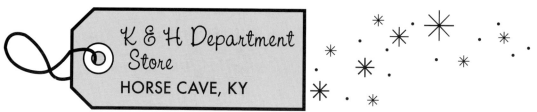

K & H Department Store
HORSE CAVE, KY

There's a store still out there, the kind your mother and grandmother used to shop at, and it's in Horse Cave.

K & H Department Store has been a staple in this small cave country town since 1972.

Founder Ken Russell says, "We cater to people who don't like to be overwhelmed by the amount of merchandise at the malls. Our patrons can still choose from such brands for the ladies as Koret, Alfred Dunner, Erica, Southern Lady, Levi jeans and LifeStride shoes."

Russell goes on to point out that men shoppers can purchase names like Hagger, Levi, Dockers, Izod, Arrow, Van Heusen andNunn Bush. Children's lines also feature top-of-the-line brands.

"There aren't many of these stores left," Russell adds. "But we have prices equal or less than the big box retailers of major chains and mall stores."

The store was originated by Ken Russell and his mother, Hilda, who formed a partnership to open K & H in 1972. The store was originally in what is now the Kentucky Repertory Theatre, but in the early 80s Ken relocated to its current location.

Russell has traveled to New York, Atlanta and Lexington to purchase clothing for his store, but admits that most of his purchases are now done in Atlanta where southern styles are more in line with what "our customers want."

His philosophy is not to try to keep up with ever-changing trends, but instead sell only the classic styles of clothing.

"I've tried to build this business on hometown values, Russell continues. "And we have folks who stop in and seem amazed to find a store like this still operating."

In 2008, Russell sold the store to new owner, Candice Eastridge, who plans to maintain the same quality service that K & H customers have enjoyed since 1972.

K & H still offers free lay-a-way, gift wrapping, tuxedo rental and dry cleaning drop-off.

You can bet there's not many of these around.

SHOPPERS INFO

Address:
103 Water Street
Hours:
9 a.m. – 5 p.m., Monday – Saturday
1 p.m. – 5 p.m., Sunday
Phone:
270/786-2562
Area Attractions:
Kentucky Repertory Theatre, Caves, Kentucky Cave & Karsts Museum

SOUTH CENTRAL

Knot-Head
SOMERSET, KY

Hats come in all styles. Some are made from many different materials, but none are like the wooden ones made by Chris Ramsey in his wood-turning shop, called Knot-Head in Somerset.

It all starts with a rough-hewn solid block of wood from a felled tree in Kentucky, and before long Ramsey has turned his so-called "blank" into a work of art.

A Knot-Head hat is considered a masterpiece, and one of Ramsey's cowboy hats is in the possession of President George W. Bush.

"It was a pleasure to welcome you to the Oval Office. Thank you for the cowboy hat," wrote the 43rd President.

The hats are actually made to wear, sized and sculptured to look like a hat made of fabric. Weighing about seven to nine ounces, the hats can be comfortably worn.

These incredible head coverings are one-of-a-kind works of art and are, once seen, must-have collector items.

Ramsey looks for special woods, even from a tree lost to weather,

disease or felled in the name of progress. From the tree he takes a single piece. With no gluing or joining of individual pieces he sets about to craft a hat like you've never seen. He takes pride in what is called thin-walled turning, with many of his works reaching an almost unheard of thickness of a mere 3/32 of an inch. Each hat has a luxurious 20-coat lacquer finish. This is followed by a final hand-rubbing process that gives the hat the desired finish.

Other styles of hats include derby, top hat, baseball cap, golf hat, lady's garden hat and a fishing hat.

Although hats are the big draw at Knot-Head's, Ramsey enjoys creating natural edge pedestal and legged bowls, and other lath turned sculptures.

SHOPPERS INFO **?**

Address:
212 Ohio Street
Hours:
By Appointment Only
Phone:
606/677-2466
Area Attractions:
Lake Cumberland

Magnolia Alley
CAMPBELLSVILLE, KY

It is only fitting that a shop named Magnolia Alley be located in a 100 year-old two story house, multiple fireplaces and fabulous chandeliers.

Kathy Bryant English owns and operates the business, but with help from her husband, daughter, sister, mom and dad, you can be sure nothing falls through the cracks here.

The shop offers a pleasant mix of trendy and traditional accessories for the home. Beautiful, functional lamps, framed pictures and paintings, elegant mirrors, colorful silk floral, and an assortment of decorative urns make this a delightful place to shop for you. Who said anything about gifts?

A recently enclosed patio is a perfect spot for presenting house plants, wind chimes, garden stepping stones and tapestry throws.

One room in the house is pretty much dedicated to a large selection of scented candles in the most current colors.

You're going to really enjoy the "dining room." Here you'll see an array of fine china, crystal, aluminum serving pieces, and everyday stoneware. Some of the brands include Lenox, Gorham, Godinger, Fiesta, Badash Crystal, and Crystal Clear.

A large add-on in the back of the original house is where Kathy operates her florist portion of Magnolia Alley. This is where fresh flowers and silk arrangements are prepared.

"Our flower

shop is full-service," says Kathy. "Whatever the need or occasion."

Like so many of the wonderful shops across Kentucky, Magnolia Alley really gets into the Holiday Season. Each room takes on a different theme in preparation for the third Thursday in October, preview open house.

Campbellsville is just another little community in Kentucky blessed with some good shopping.

SHOPPERS INFO ?

Address:
411 East Main Street
Hours:
9 a.m. – 6 p.m., Monday – Friday
9 a.m. – 5 p.m., Saturday
Phone:
888/762-3988
Area Attractions:
Green River Lake

Moore's Shoe Store
CAMPBELLSVILLE, KY

ost of the towns in Kentucky are small. With the exception of Louisville and Lexington, and sprinkling of medium size cities, the state features quite a few "small town USA's."

And that's the fun part of actually discovering some really unique places to shop.

Campbellsville, in Taylor County, has one such store that is as solid as a rock.

In February 1961, 19-year-old Buddy Moore opened a shoe store at 103 South Central Avenue. Almost 48 years later Buddy and the store are going strong.

Moore's Shoes is one of those types of stores that has become somewhat of an icon in Campbellsville. It's a hub of activity, not only selling shoes to customers who come from miles away, but also a place to discuss some of the hot topics of the day.

It's common for Buddy to be in his store six days a week from 9 a.m. until 5 p.m.

Boxes and shoes are everywhere. They are Red Wings, cowboy boots, Florsheims and numerous other brands customers are trying on.

"The amazing thing about our store," offers wife Roberta, "is that we have many customers who don't know the sizes of family members when they come in

to shop, but Buddy knows. It seems he never forgets a customer and his favorite style or size."

It's not surprising as long as he has been in the business what all Buddy knows about shoes and peoples feet.

He is a very talented shoe repairman, but what you may not know is he is trained in orthopedic prescription work and serves several doctors and their patients.

The downtown store has been referred to as a downtown landmark by some, while others from miles around refer to it as a good place to buy shoes.

SHOPPERS INFO ?

Address:
103 South Central Avenue
Hours:
9 a.m. - 5 p.m., Monday - Friday
9 a.m. - 3 p.m., Saturday
Closed Sunday
Phone:
270/789-2227
Area Attractions:
Green River Lake

This is one place you can't drive past without stopping. Even if it's a spin through the parking lot, you ask yourself, "What the heck is going on here?"

For years, owners, John and Sebrina Erskine have been collectors of funky junk and art, and when they opened Paradise Point some two years ago out in the "middle of nowhere", it quickly became an oasis for lakeside shopping.

Located only a couple of minutes from Barren River State Resort Park, between Scottsville and Glasgow, the ultra-hip business takes on multiple personalities. It's a furniture store. It's a restaurant. Or is it a good place to relax and people watch?

The truth is, it's a little of each.

Where do John and Sebrina come up with all of this stuff? From retro barware, old luggage, 50s and 60s furniture, campy vintage décor,

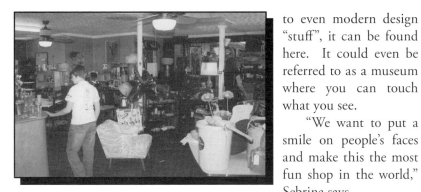

to even modern design "stuff", it can be found here. It could even be referred to as a museum where you can touch what you see.

"We want to put a smile on people's faces and make this the most fun shop in the world," Sebrina says.

Inside or out, depending on the weather, John likes to oversee Harry's Weiner Shack, which he says are the best hot dogs on the planet. When he gets through topping it off with relishes, onions, peppers or chili, you'll quickly want to find one of the patio tables to sit down and enjoy.

For dessert or take-home there's fresh baked treats, Fiji water or Bongo Java coffee, as well as gourmet cooking products and lots of unusual snacks.

SHOPPERS INFO

Address:
10300 New Glasgow Road, 31-E
Hours:
Open: April through Labor Day, Friday, Saturday & Sunday only.
Hours: When we get there, till we get tired (9 a.m. – 5 p.m.)
Phone:
270/392-0465
Area Attractions:
Barren River State Park

Paul's Discount
SOMERSET, KY

Joe Neikirk, owner of Paul's Discount in Somerset, is well-aware that his store is somewhat of a dinosaur by retail store standards.

The 20,000 square foot store, in today's computer age, still uses price tags at the checkout.

Paul's opened in 1960 as a small army surplus store, selling furniture, coal furnaces, and fishing and hunting supplies. As business grew, so did the store structurally. Bigger rooms were added and so was merchandise.

The store is known for its "slightly" disorganized décor, with items routinely stacked from the concrete floor to the ceiling. "Paul's Everyday Low Prices" has been the store's motto for over 48 years.

This is one of those stores so unique that when you visit you'll see things you probably didn't know you needed. There's a good chance you'll leave with it.

Fabric and sewing supplies, plumbing, men's and ladies clothing,

hunting and fishing products, auto supplies, home and auto electrical parts, hardware for home and farm, and water sport toys for the lake.

"Because of all the hardware and outdoor sports products, Paul's has been dubbed the 'men's mall'," says Neikirk.

To further emphasize how unusual the store is, the store's thirty employees do not wear uniforms, smocks or aprons, a human voice answers the phone when called, (it's still the original number they were assigned back in 1960), and they still close on Sunday.

When you leave Paul's, its common to hear a friendly voice telling you, "don't work too hard and thanks for shopping at Paul's."

SHOPPERS INFO

Address:
1616 Hwy. 2227
Hours:
8 a.m. - 9 p.m., Monday - Saturday
Phone:
606/678-4405
Area Attractions:
Lake Cumberland

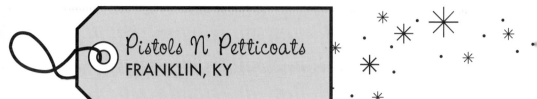
For a small store in a small town to be going strong after thirty years, it must be doing something right.

That's the case of Pistols N' Petticoats, a children's shop located right in the heart of downtown Franklin, Kentucky.

Owner, Karen Hester, has always had a simple philosophy when it comes to doing business. "We try to treat people the way we like to be treated, with kindness and a friendly smile," she says.

But here, there's much more than smiles. There's also top quality merchandise at value prices.

Stride Rite and Born shoes, Angel, Lamour, Ralph Lauren, Willets, Kissy Kissy, Letop, Willbeth, Wes and Willie and Biscotti are all top-notch brands.

Pistols N' Petticoats can outfit newborns all the way to size 16 in clothing for both boys and girls.

Some 4,000 square foot of retail area displays the clothing, as well as baby beds and bedding, gifts, toys, jewelry and stuffed animals.

"We get customers from all over the surrounding area including Tennessee," says Karen. "And we'll get people in here even from the Carolinas, Arizona and California."

When you visit Pistols N' Petticoats there's a chance you will meet Sweetie, Karen's rat terrier. She likes to greet the little ones, and might even hang out with them in the little playhouse where there's an assortment of toys to keep them all occupied while mom shops.

It's only fitting that so many children are a part of this 100 year old building that once was the Franklin post office, a newspaper office, law office, hardware store, and even a grocery. They are building their memories of coming here just like many of their parents did…and still do.

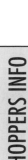

SHOPPERS INFO

Address:
120 W. Kentucky Avenue
Hours:
9 a.m. – 5 p.m., Monday – Saturday
Closed Sunday
Phone:
270/586-5210
Area Attractions:
Kentucky Downs

SOUTH CENTRAL

a bakery in a shopping book? You better believe it. Makes sense to me. In fact I can't think of many other places I'd rather shop.

Riley's has been turning out mouth-watering baked goodies in Bowling Green since 1943, first in the downtown area on historic Fountain Square, and then at their present location since 1970, on 31-W By-Pass.

I remember as a small child, on a stroll around the block with my grandmother, it was not complete without a stop to look in the front window at all of those cakes and cookies. I always hoped and she always said, "Well, let's go in and see what we can find."

For me it was always the same, a delicious cream horn, coated in white powdered sugar, which I proceeded to get all over the front of my shirt. But it didn't matter to me or my grandmother, because it was worth it.

Riley's Bakery is an experience. From the moment you walk through the front door and step into an inviting reception area, you're not sure

which way to turn. The large glass cases are packed with almost every baked goodie you can imagine.

Cakes, pies, cobblers, breads, rolls, donuts, puffs, brownies, are all like magnets pulling at you to stop their way. This is one place, no matter what you buy, you can't go wrong.

Owner Dan Riley takes pride in continuing what his dad, Bill started, and now son Sean is following in the same tradition.

For an independent bakery to be a force in a town like Bowling Green for over 65 years it has to be good. And it is.

Even though there could be a short wait, depending on the time of day, you won't have to wait long. A courteous staff moves quickly in filling the orders. They really do seem to enjoy their job. But who wouldn't?

When you go, take your time. Browse through every case. And all the while you can look through the large glass window behind the counter, and see the pastry chefs in their baker whites scurrying about decorating cakes, icing brownies or placing racks of bread in the giant ovens.

Let's see give me one of those, two of those, a dozen of those, oh well, you know the procedure.

SHOPPERS INFO

Address:
819 31-W By-Pass
Hours:
6:45 a.m. – 5:30 p.m., Monday – Friday
6:45 a.m. – 2:30 p.m., Saturday
Phone:
270/842-7636
Area Attractions:
National Corvette Museum, Beech Bend Park, Lost River Cave, Western Kentucky University

SOUTH CENTRAL

Southern Outdoor Furniture
AUBURN, KY

Y ou can't travel along Rt. 68/80 around Auburn without noticing Southern Outdoor Furniture.

It sits on the outskirts of town, between Russellville and Bowling Green, and without question it has one of the largest selections of outdoor furniture anywhere, and I mean anywhere. The area surrounding the store is full of wrought iron and aluminum tables and chairs, gazebos, sheds, swings, arbors and gliders. These selections are many.

This is a family-owned business that started in 1993. In the beginning the small shop built furniture. Brothers Steve and Kevin Miller, from a local Mennonite community, soon outgrew their place, and in 1997 they moved into their 7,400 square foot facility. Not long after, their dad Joe was onboard with them as they put more emphasis on strictly retail. Now the entire building is showroom space that has allowed them to stock wicker and rattan sunroom furnishings, as well as increasing their inventory of Amish-built bedroom, dining, office, and living room furniture. The store also sells wooden outdoor furniture from Ohio Amish builders, maintenance free poly, and outdoor wicker.

Southern Outdoor Furniture is a high quality

store. A huge selection of cushions and umbrellas can be coordinated with any purchase, and most of their merchandise can be customized as far as wood choices, stains and fabrics are concerned.

"We represent twenty-five Amish builders," says Bob Miller. "And we carry good names like Lloyd Flanders, Telescope, Casual, Classic Cushion, Hanamint, Chicago Wicker and Classic."

The Millers say they sell throughout Kentucky and Tennessee, with some sales going all the way to Texas.

SOUTH CENTRAL

SHOPPERS INFO

Address:
U.S. Hwy. 68/80
Hours:
8 a.m. – 5 p.m., Monday – Saturday
Phone:
1-888/778-4748
270/542-7223
Area Attraction:
Shaker Museum

Steve's Sports Cards
BOWLING GREEN, KY

What started out as strictly a baseball card store back in 1986 has turned into a full-fledged sports card shop.

Naturally, baseball cards are a big chunk of Steve Kissinger's business, but basketball and football card collectors have also made their presence known. At Steve's Sports Cards, enthusiast can have a field day searching through the thousands of cards on display.

Like many of us, Steve had been a collector since he was a kid, but after giving it up for a few years, he began to get serious again when he went to college at Western Kentucky University.

"Several years ago there may have been 40 to 50 sports card shops in Kentucky," Kessinger says. "But today I'd say that number might be down to 10 to 15."

Steve's Sports Cards has cards that date back to 1887 up to the current players.

And how much do some of these cards cost?

"I have cards for as little as a penny all the way up to a 1933 Babe Ruth card for $5,000," he says. "I also have many different unopened packs and complete sets as far back as 1981."

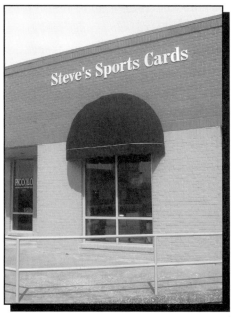

The store also carries rookie cards, and the relatively new jersey cards. These are cards that have an actual piece of a players jersey attached to the card.

Card collectors can also find collecting supplies here

that enable the cards to be stored and protected properly.

A couple of decades ago the sports cards business moved from kids to adults, when it was realized some of these cards had value. But still this is something a father and son can do together for a lifetime.

As an added bonus, customers at Steve's can see his "for sale" collection of political campaign buttons.

"I collect these and sell them," he offers. "Some are as far back as 1896 all the way up to 2008."

Even though the address is on 31-W By-Pass, Steve's shop actually sits behind the front of the building. Just a little tricky getting in.

SHOPPERS INFO

?

Address:
661 U.S. 31-W By-Pass
Hours:
10 a.m. – 5 p.m., Monday – Saturday
Closed Sunday
Phone:
270/843-0183
Area Attractions:
National Corvette Museum, Lost River Cave, Beech Bend Park

The Klassic Shop
ALBANY, KY

*W*ho said a big city business couldn't be located in a little town?

Albany, KY, population 6,500 in Clinton County near the Kentucky-Tennessee line, is a good example of what shopping can be across this state.

There are fantastic little shops where you least expect to find them. I've found one here!

For more than 25 years, the Sewell's, Jack and Frances, have built The Klassic Shop into an outstanding lady's shop that sells fine clothing, accessories, jewelry, shoes and gifts.

"We make four or five buying trips a year," says Frances. "We look for fashions for our store's VIPs as well as merchandise to appeal to new customers."

Don't get the impression that this is a snobby shop just because Frances buys for her VIPs. It's because she does indeed have customers who travel quite a distance for her top-of-the-line clothing, and she wants to meet their expectations.

The Sewells are proud of the fact that their daughter Melissa has come into the business and even granddaughter, Kiley, has shown an interest. With this said, it looks like The Klassic Shop will only continue to get even better.

Some of the lines include Berek, Liz Claiborne, City Girl, Tribal, Focus and 600 West. Melissa likes to point out that shoes and handbag brands will vary by season. "It's whoever has the most unique styles," she says.

"My husband asked me when I was going to retire," laughed Frances. "I told him I hope never, as I am doing what I love."

And that's the attitude that prevails in this shop. Because of this and the incredible selection, it's easy to see why customers come from several states, including Ohio and Florida, to this little town with the big city store.

SHOPPERS INFO ?

Address:
114 Washington Street
Hours:
9 a.m. - 5 p.m., Monday - Friday
9 a.m. - 3 p.m., Saturday
Closed Sunday
Phone:
606/387-5112
Area Attractions:
Dale Hollow Lake, Cumberland Lake

V & R Enterprises
BROWNSVILLE, KY

*Y*ou've got to hunt a little for V & R Enterprises, but the effort will be worth it.

Virginia and Ronnie Rountree have located their business definitely off the beaten path in Edmondson County on the outskirts of Brownsville, about 15 miles from Bowling Green.

The little warehouse might not be much to look at on the outside, but once you get inside it won't matter. Virginia promotes her shop as a "women's only warehouse."

"We are wholesalers of better women's first quality clothing," she says. "And sell for 50% to 80% off."

Designer fashions, jewelry and handbags from New York and California fill the shelves and hang from the racks here, and Virginia points out that she personally selects everything she carries in her shop.

"Our customers enjoy shopping with us knowing that not every department store carries what we do," says Virginia. "So they feel special knowing they won't see themselves coming and going."

V & R has what they call "special occasion" outfits for weddings, anniversaries, cruises or vacations.

Suits, dresses, separates, sportswear, skirt sets, handbags, jewelry and shoes comprise most of the inventory, with clothing sizes ranging from sizes two to twenty-six.

The store is open year round,

and closed only when the Rountree's are on buying trips twice a year.

"We have hundreds of ladies who shop at their convenience after we notify them," Virginia adds. "We contact customers and they like the fact they can make an appointment and come in. We try to accommodate everyone's schedule."

V & R Enterprises also carry several lines of natural health and beauty products, skin care and cosmetics as well as Shaklee vitamins and herbal products.

One of the shoe lines sold here is Dansko shoes. They are handmade in Denmark and Italy, and Virginia says "these are shoes that provide 'all day comfort' and are recommended by foot specialists."

Get to 31-W Hwy, turn on Hwy. 101 toward Brownsville, and go to Hwy. 70 (Mammoth Cave Road) turn right. Travel 3.2 miles and you are there.

SHOPPERS INFO

Address:
3376 Mammoth Cave Road, Hwy. 70
Hours:
10 a.m. – 6 p.m., Wednesday – Friday
9 a.m. – 5 p.m., Saturday
Other times by appointment
Phone:
270/597-2112
Area Attractions:
Mammoth Cave National Park

Wild Bird and Nature Store
BOWLING GREEN, KY

You can travel from one end of Kentucky to the other and very few stores, if any, match Wild Bird and Nature Store's inventory when it comes to "backyard birding."

Jeftie and Gerry Sawyer opened their store in 1999, and have continually scoured the country to bring in the best and most unusual merchandise possible for their customers.

"Being an independent shop enables us to carry any kind of bird feeder, bird house and specialty seed we mix for our customers," says Jeftie.

This is a store you can really spend some time in, especially if you are fairly new to the bird business.

"We have a staff that is very knowledgeable and can help the rookie or the pro bird watcher," she adds.

Droll Yankee, Aspects, Perky Pet, Woodlink, Bird's Choice, Coveside, and Looker are just some of the named feeders stocked here.

Squirrel feeders and mix as well as other wildlife blends that attract various wildlife to a yard can also be purchased.

Supplies for summer and winter watering can be found here in the way of misters, fountains, drippers, recirculating bird baths and heated bird baths for the colder months.

"We feel the most important thing you can provide for the birds in the winter is water, especially when everything is frozen," Jeftie said.

The garden section of the store displays art, wind chimes and lots of bird books.

Something unique to Wild Bird and Nature Store is their annual Herb Festival held the third weekend of each April. The event's main focus is on providing perennials and herbs that will attract birds and butterflies to a garden.

"We get bird lovers from all over Kentucky, Tennessee, Alabama, Arkansas and Georgia in for the festival," said Jeftie.

Throughout the year the store offers numerous seminars on techniques to attract certain types of birds.

SHOPPERS INFO

Address:
901 Lehman Avenue
Hours:
9:30 a.m. – 5 p.m., Monday – Friday
10 a.m. – 4 p.m., Saturday
Phone:
270/746-0203
Area Attractions:
National Corvette Museum, Lost River Cave, Railway Museum & Depot, Beech Bend Park

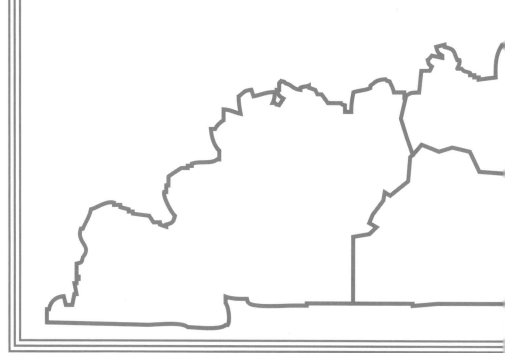

BRUCE'S GROCERY	MASON, KY
CHRISTIAN'S KINDER LADEN	COVINGTON, KY
KENTUCKY STATE PARK GIFT SHOPS	STATEWIDE (PAGE 34)
LOVE ME KNOTS HOT SOFT PRETZELS	BELLEVUE, KY
MOTCH JEWELERS	COVINGTON, KY
OLD WASHINGTON HISTORIC DISTRICT	MAYSVILLE, KY
OTTOMAN IMPORTS	COVINGTON, KY
SCHNEIDER'S SWEET SHOP	BELLEVUE, KY
THE QUILT BOX	DRY RIDGE, KY
ZEPPELIN THREADS	CYNTHIANA, KY

NORTHERN REGION

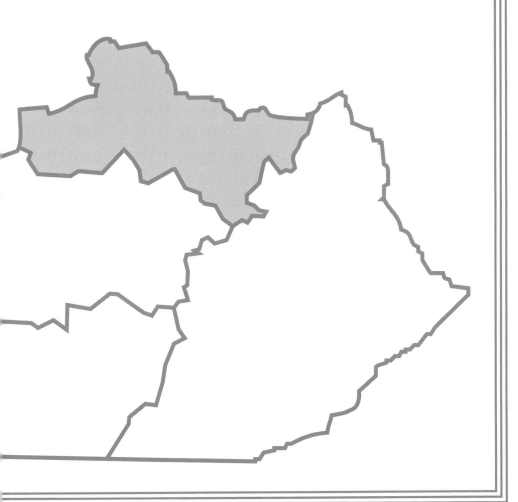

Bruce's Grocery
MASON, KY

$\mathcal{L}$ee and Scott Bruce just do what comes natural to them. They operate Bruce's Grocery, which by the way is much more than a grocery. They learned the business from their father who learned it from his.

This unpretentious building located in the small community of Mason, between Williamstown and Corinth, is a daily hub of activity as it serves customers from Grant County as well as nearby counties Harrison, Pendleton, Scott and Owen.

Bruce's Grocery is a pretty good size store with a top-quality fresh meat department, groceries, seeds, hardware, electrical, plumbing and building supplies, clothing, shoes, film development and garden items. In fact there's a saying around these parts, "if you can't find it anywhere else, go to Bruce's."

Kelly Bruce, Lee and Scott's dad, dropped out of college back in 1951 to take over for his dad who originally started the store in 1936.

So this what-ever-you-want-to-call-it-store, that sells almost everything known to man, is well over 70 years old and still going strong.

How has it managed to survive when even large grocery store chains have fallen by the wayside? How has it been able to thrive in spite of the mega centers?

According to the Bruce brothers, the answer is right there in front of them. They really do care about their customers. They not only talk the talk, but walk the walk.

"Treating the customer with respect," they say. "Making the extra effort to order what they want if we don't have it, and getting to know our customers."

Bruce's customers know this and it is their loyalty that has kept this unique store going. Many are in and out of the store two or three times a day.

Joe White is an employee at the store. He's not just any employee though. He came to work just out of high school, and almost 40 years later he's still here.

That's the kind of atmosphere we're talking about.

NORTHERN

Christian's Kinder Laden
COVINGTON, KY

Several years ago when Deb Enneking couldn't find what she considered a quality gift for her young grandson, she decided to do something about it. She opened her own shop.

Christian's Kinder Laden is located in the very popular Mainstrasse section of Covington. Her grandson, Christian, is the stores namesake for the shop that translates to "children's store."

Deb gives her husband, Steve, credit of giving the store its dollhouse look.

"It looks like a Victorian dollhouse," she says. "It is so inviting to visitors."

And how many times do you go into a store and are greeted with "you can touch and play with anything." Children are encouraged to play and explore here.

Deb likes to say that every time a child is born so is a grandmother. And now, that grandmother has a great place to shop. You will find things here that aren't in much larger shops or malls. Deb prides herself in searching out the really unusual, unique things for grandmothers to buy. Toy fairs throughout the country, and lots of time online, allow her to be very selective in what she stocks on her shelves.

The store offers an extensive line of Melissa & Doug toys, including doll houses and furniture. Oppenheim Toy Award Winners: Thomas the Train; a wide variety of puzzles; Robeez shoes from newborn to

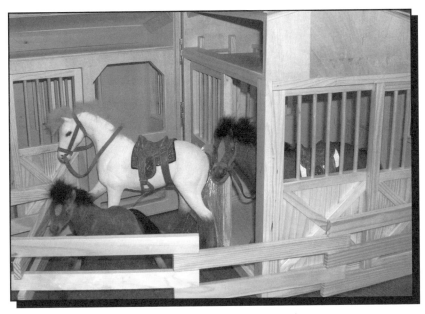

toddlers; nursery clocks and themed clocks; and Zutano clothing are just some of the quality items.

Christian's Kinder Laden also has First Communion dresses and Christening gowns.

You've got to give Deb Enneking credit when she sets out to do something, she does it. She didn't want any other grandparents going through what she did.

On the surface her store is for children, but not really. What it is is a store for grandmothers. That's okay, too.

SHOPPERS INFO

?

Address:
625 Main Street
Hours:
10 a.m. – 6 p.m., Tuesday – Friday
10 a.m. – 5 p.m., Saturday
Closed Sunday & Monday
Phone:
859/261-3655
Area Attractions:
Newport Aquarium

Love Me Knots
Hot Soft Pretzels
BELLEVUE, KY

You can be sure there's not another pretzel shop in this book, and I'll even go a step further. There may not be another pretzel shop quite like Love Me Knots in the entire country.

Call it divine intervention, luck, or good timing on how owners Janie Coleman and Jacque Newman hooked up to start this business back in 2003. It was probably a little of each, but I can tell you the pretzel world is better off for it.

Today their small shop in Bellevue is a sight for hungry eyes. The customer area is painted in "cupcake colors" with a black and white tiled floor. The pinks, blues and greens give the space an old soda fountain look. With a counter and several stools customers are drawn to sit down with a smile and order up one of the eight varieties of hot soft pretzels.

If you've never been to a pretzel shop you're in for a treat. Janie and Jacques pretzels come in several sizes, from plate-sized to the signature one ounce Love Me Knots.

Jalapeno-cheddar pretzels and cinnamon-sugar glaze dessert pretzels are two of the most popular.

Now get this! You can build-your own hot soft pretzel sandwich us-

ing a variety of meats, cheeses, veggies, and different condiments. Side items are cheese dip, cream cheese and glaze.

Customers who come to Love Me Knots can even add another dimension to their desire to take pretzels home. A variety of frozen pretzels ready to bake, in packs of ten all the way up to packs of 100 Love Me Knots are ready for caryout. And if that's not enough, you can buy take-home pretzel mix kits.

Love Me Knots Hot Soft Pretzels have become so popular in the northern Kentucky area that the Cincinnati Reds are now selling their product at all of their home games. And, in addition, a major national grocery chain is testing their market.

I will tell you this: a pretzel is not a pretzel until you've eaten one of these.

SHOPPERS INFO

Address:
182 Covert Run Pike
Hours:
10 a.m. – 5 p.m., Monday – Friday
12 noon – 5 p.m., Saturday
Closed Sunday
Phone:
859/781-6569
Area Attractions:
Mainstrasse Village, Newport Aquarium

Motch Jewelers
COVINGTON, KY

For over 150 years Motch Jewelers has been selling top quality merchandise, excellent value and exceptional service in downtown Covington.

In 1857 Michael Motch, who had arrived in America from France, opened a little shop that is still being talked about today, although it is no longer a little shop.

At the time Motch opened his shop, Covington was a city of 10,000 people and already had eight jewelry stores. This was three years, mind you, before the start of the Civil War.

The store became a success, and before long outgrew its location. Motch hired a prominent Cincinnati architect to design his "new store" at 613 Madison Avenue, and that's where it has been since 1871.

Today, those same classy walnut jewelry cases, a 12-foot high George Jones regulator clock with an eagle and American flag pendulum, are very

prominent in the store's showroom. A landmark Boston E. Howard & Company street clock sits on the sidewalk in front of the store, where it has been for the last 132 years.

Today Motch's is a full service jewelry store offering custom design, and buyers and sellers of estate jewelry.

Gemologist Tim Dwight is a qualified estate appraiser, one of only 60 in the United States. This shouldn't surprise anyone, but Motch Jewelers is a charter member of the National Association of Jewelry Appraisers. It's no wonder the store has a beautiful selection of Victorian jewelry for sale.

Motch takes pride in its ability to repair and restore jewelry and watches to the highest of standards. They do this by continually educating their staff on the latest of anything that has to do with jewelry.

Diamonds set in platinum or 14 kt. Gold, Colombian emerald rings and necklaces, and gemstones of ruby, sapphire and amethyst can be custom designed. One of the store's cases shows off a variety of pearls, from Chinese backwater to the black Tahitian multi-colored strand necklace. Waterford crystal, Reed & Barton silver, and Seth Thomas clocks are a staple of the store.

NORTHERN

SHOPPERS INFO

?

Address:
613 Madison Avenue
Hours:
9:30 a.m. - 4:45 p.m., Monday - Friday
9:30 a.m. - 2:45 p.m., Saturday
Closed Sunday
Phone:
859/431-1745
Area Attractions:
Mainstrasse, Newport Aquarium

Old Washington
Historic District
MAYSVILLE, KY

It's almost like a book on shopping in Kentucky couldn't be written without including one of the state's oldest shopping districts.

Old Washington on the outskirts of Maysville in Mason County, was a pioneer village settled in 1786, and in the early 1800s it became one of the top shopping towns in all of Kentucky. History says the shopping was so good that even people from Lexington would visit Washington to shop. It must have been good, because back then that was no easy feat. Considering the roadways in a horse-and-wagon, it took awhile.

What is so unique is that more than 200 years later people are still finding Old Washington a good place to shop.

The charming community is worth a visit if you do nothing but stroll the sidewalks and breathe in the historic ambiance of the surroundings.

The village is actually located in the south end of Maysville just off

U.S. 68. It is considered one of the largest antique shopping villages in Northern Kentucky.

Over 20 antiques and specialty shops, housed in nine buildings along Old Main Street, make for an enjoyable day of browsing and shopping.

Phyllis' Antique Lamp Shop has a little bit of everything. Of course lamps, but also chandeliers, shades, Civil War swords, hatpins, and too much to even list. You'll spend some time here.

Keepsake Treasures offers a variety of antiques, furniture, glassware, jewelry and books.

Other shops include the Carousel Shop, a shop for horses off carousels, Victorian furniture, and a carriage museum. Then there is The Strawberry Vine, The Lamb's Ear, The Strawberry Patch, Bertland Shop, The Gray Wolf Antiques, David's Brass Works, Elaine's Gallery & Framing, Washington Hall Antiquities, The Shade Spot, The Side Door, Buffalo Trail Antiques, Stella's Stuff, The Old Curiosity Shop and Spellbound.

One of the shops in Old Washington is named Rob Weingartner. Often visitors can watch as he works in gold, sterling and stones. He offers one-of-a-kind pieces for sale.

Another thing that makes this place user friendly is the public restrooms and water fountain available at the Washington Meeting House.

NORTHERN

SHOPPERS INFO

Address:
U.S. 68
Hours:
Store hours, and days open, vary
Phone:
606/759-7423
Area Attractions:
Maysville

Ottoman Imports
COVINGTON, KY

There is proof in Covington, Kentucky that a little place can make a big noise.

Located in the Mainstrasse Village in the historic area of town, Ottoman Imports has made a major impact by utilizing its 350 square foot space to the fullest.

The small, colorful store is truly unique in that everything it merchandises is imported.

"What we sell will not be found anywhere else in the area, and in some cases, not in the United States," says owner Kim Maius.

Ottoman Imports has a stylish selection of handmade jewelry, pashminas, women's apparel, handbags and the accessories to go with them.

Kim travels to places like Thailand, Japan, China, and Turkey and throughout Europe in order to stock her little shop. Everything she buys is personally chosen by her and bought here.

As a former travel agent, her connections have paid off. Because of the way she buys, she is able to bring back many one-of-a-kind items that can be sold to her customers at great prices.

"I travel two to three times a year," she says. "And our prices are more than competitive."

One customer said that she and her friends love coming in the shop. "We are here often," she said. "And the prices are great."

The Mainstrasse area is a fun, entertaining section of Covington. Lots and lots of shops and res-

taurants. If you do nothing else, make sure you at least stick your head in the door at Ottoman Imports. It's a safe bet if you do that, the colorful décor will pull you the rest of the way in.

There may be a few, but very few in Kentucky that offer merchandise of this quality and styles from the four corners of the globe.

SHOPPERS INFO

Address:
603 Main Street
Hours:
11 a.m. – 6 p.m., Wednesday – Saturday
12 noon – 5 p.m., Sunday
Phone:
859/291-9555
Area Attractions:
Newport Aquarium

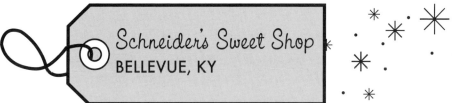

Schneider's Sweet Shop
BELLEVUE, KY

Schneider's Sweet Shop in Bellevue has become a local icon at its 420 Fairfield Avenue location. Opened in 1939 by Robert Schneider and is wife, Lill, the shop was one of those old-fashioned neighborhood candy and ice cream shops.

Using his years of experience, time-tested recipes, and high quality ingredients, Robert and his family built the business into what it is today.

Jack Schneider, Robert's son, took over the operation in 1986. He had worked alongside his dad for over 20 years, and he and his wife Kathy have continued to put out a sweet product that people come from miles around to buy.

"Our most popular item is and has been our Opera Creams," offers Jack Schneider. "This candy is unique to Northern Kentucky. You don't find this anywhere else."

This candy is so good! Made with pure rich cream, it is the ultimate of cream candy.

The pecan Carmelettes, sometime known as turtles, are also incredible. Made from Georgia pecans, layered with rich creamy caramel, covered in rich, delicious milk chocolate, this tasty sweet is not only purchased over the counter but shipped to customers all over the country.

Schneider's Sweet Shop only makes three flavors of fudge: chocolate, vanilla

and peanut butter, but what they make is fantastic.

They also turn out sugar free milk and dark chocolate cordial cherries, truffles, carmellows, turtles, caramels, and mint patties.

As a bonus when you visit Schneider's, they also sell homemade ice cream. Their soda fountain serves up delicious malts, shakes, floats, sundaes and banana splits.

What more can you ask for? An awesome candy store that sells homemade ice cream!

Schneider's Sweet Shop is one of those wonderful shops that has been doing it the right way for almost 70 years.

SHOPPERS INFO ?

Address:
420 Fairfield Avenue
Hours:
10 a.m. - 9 p.m., Monday - Saturday
Phone:
859/431-3545
Area Attractions:
Newport Aquarium, History, Mainstrasse Village

The Quilt Box
DRY RIDGE, KY

When you have a name like The Quilt Box, and you sell quilts, you'd better be good.

And it is.

A trip to Natalie Lahner's quilt shop is part of the fun experience of getting there. Once you spot the sign on Ky. 467 and travel the half-mile gravel lane, upon arriving you may just want to get out and look around before entering the restored 150-year-old cabin that serves as The Quilt Box. There's a pond, garden, and even a fenced area with all kinds of farm animals from horses, goats, sheep and a few peacocks. And at some point on this trip you're sure to see Furguson the cat.

Let's say that once inside you quickly recognize that this is a serious quilt shop. *Better Homes and Gardens American Patchwork & Quilting Magazine* has named The Quilt Box as one of the top 10 quilting shops in America.

Natalie has created a fun-like masterpiece with her cluster of

rooms, and some of the best lighting you've ever seen for picking out colors. She has in excess of 5,000 bolts of fabric in every color imaginable.

"We carry mostly 100% cotton fabric made for quilting," Natalie says. "There's a few other fabrics, you know, some cutesy stuff used mostly for clothing."

Natalie is quick to point out that it was her fascination with her grandmother's quilting that peaked her interest. In fact, she has her grandmother's quilt box that inspired the naming of her shop.

This shop carries any and every quilting accessory known to man. Kits for various projects and supplies required to finish the quilt are the norm here.

Natalie says that today quilting is easy. "Now everyone is doing it on a machine," she adds. "With a machine, they can complete a quilt in a week."

"Hand-quilters" are getting more difficult to find, according to Natalie. She says most are elderly and that soon it could become a lost art.

The Quilt Box offers classes in both hand and machine quilting.

SHOPPERS INFO

Address:
Ky. Highway 467
(Three miles from I-75 exit 159)
Hours:
9:30 a.m. – 5 p.m., Monday – Saturday
Closed Sunday
Phone:
859/824-4007
Area Attractions:
Barkers Blackberry Hill Winery

Zeppelin Threads
CYNTHIANA, KY

Zeppelin Threads is an unusual quilt shop in a 200 year-old Federal style historic house in downtown Cynthiana.

It's unusual in several ways. First the owner.

Usually quilting is associated with the older generations, you know, the so-called senior citizens. But here the shop owner is only 31-years-old.

Heather Ladick is proof that passion and a strong willingness to learn, can overcome the fact that she is young by quilting standards.

"I've actually been sewing since I was nine," she says. "I had a step-mother who was really into sewing and exposed me to it."

But the quilting aspect, particularly the hand-quilting, came about for her efforts to learn the fading lost art.

"It's a connection to the past," Heather says. "I know the trend is machine quilting, but we are really fortunate to have quite a few hand quilters in our area."

The name Zeppelin Threads came about because of Heather and husband Ben's affection for airships. "I know it's kind of an unusual name, but we liked it," she offered.

This small attractive shop is absolutely full to its 14-foot ceilings with all kinds of unique prints, solid lines, and organic fabrics, as well as a wide range of notions and patterns.

"I don't carry a single item I don't stand behind, or fabric that I wouldn't

want to wrap myself in and sleep under," Heather boldly states.

Ben, her husband, is a woodworker and has put his special touch in the shop. The original refinished floors, the beautiful milled popular shelves, and the walls, painted a rich, historic purple, all add up to a most attractive place to shop.

This shop is really a breath of fresh air in that there is someone as young as this owner who is on a mission to make sure people in Kentucky have a chance to carry on the tradition of hand quilting.

She is adamant about wanting her shop to reflect hand quilting, and it does!

SHOPPERS INFO

Address:
205 S. Main Street
Hours:
10 a.m. - 6 p.m., Tuesday & Thursday
10 a.m. - 3 p.m., Wednesday, Friday & Saturday
Closed Sunday
Phone:
859/234-1802
Area Attractions:
Cynthiana County Museum

A.D. CAMPBELL COMPANY	MIDDLESBORO, KY
APPALACHIAN ARTISAN CENTER	HINDMAN, KY
BOBBY DUNCAN'S GENERAL STORE	STRUNK, KY
BYBEE POTTERY	BYBEE, KY
CAT'S PAW GIFTS & ANTIQUES	IRVINE, KY
COUNTRY AT HEART	PRESTONSBURG, KY
HOMEOWNERS HARDWARE	CUMBERLAND, KY
KENTUCKY ARTISAN CENTER	BEREA, KY
KENTUCKY STATE PARK GIFT SHOPS	STATEWIDE (PAGE 34)
LOG HOUSE CRAFT GALLERY	BEREA, KY
MICKEY'S	PIKEVILLE, KY
RED DOG & COMPANY	LONDON, KY
SWEET KREATIONS	STEARNS, KY
TATER KNOB POTTERY	BEREA, KY
THE BLACK BARN	LOMANSVILLE, KY
THE FRAME UP GALLERY	ASHLAND, KY
THE RUSTY HINGE	STAMBAUGH, KY

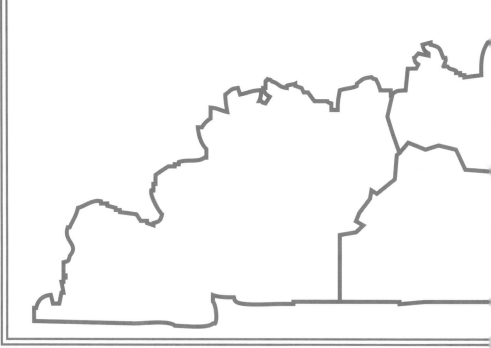

EASTERN REGION

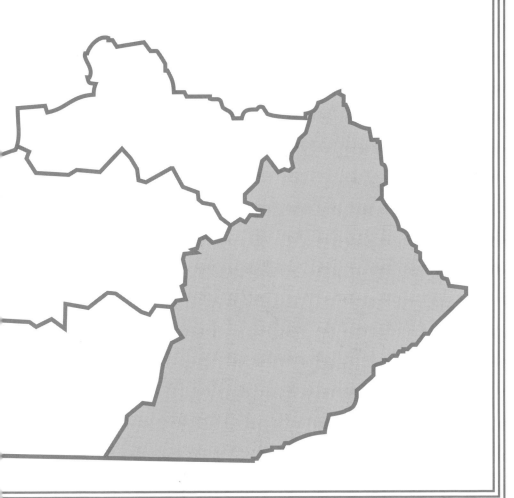

A.D. Campbell Company
MIDDLESBORO, KY

iddlesboro, Kentucky sits near the Tennessee and Virginia borders right down there in the corner of the state. Because of this location the town draws people from these two nearby states to spend money.

A special draw is A.D. Campbell Company, a women's clothing store downtown. One of the things that make this store so unique is that it has been in continuous operation since 1889 strictly as a women's store.

Owner Brenda Adams says her store draws equally from Kentucky, Tennessee and Virginia.

"We offer women a choice," she says. "We endeavor to carry different lines than the mall stores and stock only limited numbers of each item."

This store has quite a history. When Alva Douglas Campbell opened his doors for business on May 1, 1889, it was "female finery" at its best, most of which was imported from Baltimore. However, there was a dressmaker and milliner on location. The following year, though, the wooden structure burned, so when A.D. built back he did so with brick, and that same building at 2031 Cumberland Avenue has been in operation ever since.

A.D. Campbell Company has been able to survive throughout the years by service and product, offers Brenda.

"People tell me they can't find what we have at the mall," she adds. "I cater more to older wom-

en, and at the mall they don't so much. We stay away from fad items and stock more traditional clothing."

Brenda points out that the nostalgia factor still helps a lot.

"We get a lot of people here that tell me their great-grandmother or grandmother shopped here. They want to come by just to see this store," she says.

The store's long, narrow layout combined with the old worn floors and yesteryear display cases all make for a unique shopping experience.

Don't be misled into thinking this is not a first class store, because it is. It still stocks missy, petite and plus sizes, as well as Tia sweaters and Graff Sportswear.

When you stop in you can't help but feel the passion Brenda Adams has for the store.

"I started working here when I was 18 years old," she says.

SHOPPERS INFO

Address:
2031 Cumberland Avenue
Hours:
9 a.m. – 5:30 p.m., Monday – Saturday
Closed Sunday
Phone:
606/248-3625
Area Attractions:
Cumberland Gap, Pine Mountain State Resort Park

EASTERN

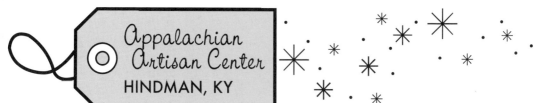

Appalachian Artisan Center
HINDMAN, KY

Hindman in Knott County is full of rich traditional Appalachian history, and though the county is full of pride, perhaps there is none greater than what they have for their local artists. At the center of it all is the Appalachian Artisan center.

Located in downtown Hindman, it has become the regional marketing and support system for artists throughout the area. From pottery to jewelry, stained glass to paintings, furniture to quilts, one-of-a-kind pieces are available for visitors to purchase. It is common for live demonstrations by jewelers and woodworkers.

Amanda Combs, one of the Center's staff says "people enjoy watching a piece of furniture emerge from good old Kentucky hardwood."

The Appalachian Artisan Center is one of those fun places to browse, and no matter how many times you visit you will see something new. The skill level of the artists and wood crafters is stunning. The construction of the rocking chairs with no nails or screws and incredible wood carvings entices you to take a close look and wonder to yourself, if not out loud, "how did they do that?"

Forty-nine counties and 150 craftsmen display their

196

products here, and all of the participants are juried.

The Center has a café for the enjoyment of shoppers. Soups and an assortment of sandwiches named after some of the icons of the area add to the uniqueness of the visit. It's hard to beat a Carr Creek Chicken Salad Sandwich or a Possum Trot Ham.

SHOPPERS INFO ?

Address:
16 West Main Street
Hours:
10 a.m. - 6 p.m., Monday - Friday
10 a.m. - 4 p.m., Saturday
Phone:
606/785-9855
Area Attractions:
Carr Creek State Park, Hindman Settlement School, Alice Lloyd College

EASTERN

ou can travel from one end of this state to the other but you will not see another store like Bobby Duncan's. Maybe similar, but that's all.

Bobby, who was born in 1928, has been working at the store since he was 17. It's safe to say that he still has a few things for sale that have been in the store as long as he has.

Stuff is literally everywhere. In the aisles, hanging from the ceiling, and on both sides of a stairway that leads to a storage area, open in the center, on the second level.

Bobby has just about anything you'll need: automotive supplies, sleds, cook wear, washboards and metal tubs, saddles and bridles, garden tools. It goes on and on to even include bread and milk.

"There was something I needed to fix an old fireplace I had," volunteered one customer. "I couldn't find it anywhere. I thought I'd see if Bobby had it. He did."

Bobby says he 'pretty much' knows where everything is. "Unless somebody has moved it on me," he says. "Then I might have to look a bit."

There is no way on earth a store like Bobby Duncan's could be inventoried.

"Back in the early 50's they audited me," Bobby said. "I even remember the man's name that was here. You know I haven't seen anyone from there since."

Geneva, his wife, comes to work with

him daily and though she says "her husband can find everything... he does lose me ever now and then."

A few of the locals sit on the front porch when it's not too cold or too hot. But when it's real cold they sit near a big Keller-Burnside stove that supplies most of the store's heat. Close by, hanging on the wall, is a Richard Nixon photo.

The picture doesn't necessarily mean Bobby's politics lean one way or the other. It just means that years ago he ended up with a picture. That's the way with things here. They've been here a while. And that's what makes Bobby Duncan's General Store a special place.

It would be safe to say that very few people in McCreary County have not been there.

SHOPPERS INFO ?

Address:
155 Strunk Highway
Hours:
8 a.m. – 6 p.m., Monday – Saturday
Closed Sunday
Phone:
606/354-2202
Area Attractions:
Big South Fork Scenic Railroad, Barthell Coal Camp

EASTERN

Bybee Pottery
BYBEE, KY

a pottery place that tracks its existence back to 1809. That's almost 200 years!

Bybee Pottery is the oldest existing pottery west of the Alleghenies, and the little community of Bybee in Madison County, near Richmond, considers this business a local landmark of days gone by.

The old log building has housed the equipment for over 100 years and has actual sales records that date back to 1845.

Not much has changed at Bybee's over the last century when it comes to producing the company's wares.

The process begins with retrieving the clay, or mining it, as it is often referred to. Then they grind it in the antique pug mill, throwing and shaping it by hand into articles of ornamental and practical use on the potter's wheel.

The clay used by Bybee's actually comes from a nearby location. According to Bybee Pottery, the clay they open-pit mine is the same clay that was mined by Kentucky's first settlers and taken to Fort Boonesborough and used for assembling their dishes.

Obviously there is a high degree of skill required to artistically craft a pleasing piece of pottery that people are willing to pay money for.

The clay, mixed with water, is ground in the old pug mill and stored in an old vault that allows it to remain moist and pliable. The clay is weighed on antique balances to make sure of uniformity. Next, the potter throws it and then shapes it into the desired form. Each piece is allowed to dry. Then it is glazed and cured in a kiln fired to 2,200 degrees. The clay has now been turned into a beautiful, functional piece of art ready for sale.

Harvey Conner has been making pottery here for just over 43 years. "When I got out of high school in 1965, my mom told me to get a job where I got paid every Friday. And I did right here, and have been here ever since."

Address:
610 Waco Loop
Hours:
8 a.m. – 3:30 p.m., Monday – Friday
Closed Saturday & Sunday
Phone:
859/369-5350
Area Attractions:
Arts and Crafts, Berea, Eastern Kentucky University

EASTERN

Childhood memories of an old shoe repair shop in downtown Irvine led Susan Radar and her husband, to open this shop in an old building that had sat vacant for some 20 years.

"I remember the smell of the leather and the cool darkness of the shop when on hot summer days, as children, we would duck inside to get a bottle of coke, a pack of peanuts, and watch the cobbler work," recalled Susan. "He was a very quiet man who never seemed to mind that we were there."

The impression it left was lasting, because years later when she decided on naming the business, it was a result of the old Cat's Paw sign on the windows beside the original front door.

Like so many family owned businesses, Cat's Paw started out small and has gradually evolved into a somewhat larger operation.

A diverse selection of antiques and collectibles is spearheaded by an array of grapevine pieces. These are items made from grapevines. Locally made, they include planters, bird cages, window panes, wreaths, magazine racks, wind mills, gazing balls and even furniture. There are even three sizes of grapevine mushrooms to choose from.

Doll houses and forts are something else unique to the

store. They, too, are made locally.

"They are primitive," Susan offers. "But I don't think you will ever see anything like them. They sure do get a lot of attention from our customers."

Quilts are another item that draws some attention. Susan says some are made "right here in Irvine, while others are brought in by area residents who know the stores reputation for selling quilts."

"There are a few new ones," Susan continues, "but most are original and old, and priced to sell."

A trip to Irvine can be a pleasant surprise. This little town that sits on the Kentucky River offers up a good place for lunch at the Cedar Village Restaurant, or an overnight at a first class bed and breakfast, Snug Hollow Farm that sits just a few miles from town.

SHOPPERS INFO ?

Address:
171 Broadway
Hours:
10 a.m. – 5 p.m., Monday, Tuesday, Thursday, Friday
10 a.m. – 4 p.m., Saturday
Closed Wednesday & Sunday
Phone:
606/726-9940
Area Attractions:
Berea Crafts

EASTERN

Country At Heart
PRESTONSBURG, KY

The name is a little misleading. If a person just looks at the name, it really doesn't give a hint to all of the really good things inside their doors.

I've always said the things travelers and tourists really like to do is shop and eat. At Country At Heart you can do both.

As of late, the shop has added to its name Old Town Fudge Company, and for good reason.

"We are known for our many delicious flavors of homemade fudge," says Jan Wells, who along with husband Ken opened this downtown Prestonsburg business in 1997.

Some of those flavors Jan is talking about are Key Lime Cheesecake, sherbet, apple pie and pumpkin pie. Now remember, these are fudge flavors. I had never had any of these before. I have now!

The shop started out as an arts and craft store, but a couple of years

ago they figured out the shopping and eating thing.

Gourmet coffee and tea, and even an espresso bar, along with several specialty drinks have become quite popular here. Coffee drinks, smoothies, Italian sodas, and gourmet teas from The Republic of Tea are all sold here. Coffees are sold whole bean or ground.

An assortment of lunch sandwiches and a soup of the day are the usual. Most of the items on the menu have been named after friends "who gave us the recipes." Miss Ditty's Bread Pudding with Bourbon Sauce sounds interesting.

Country At Heart has several Kentucky-made guitars for sale as well as antique pieces, quilts, prints, books, candles and Blue Mountain greeting cards.

This is a fun store to visit, and if Ken is there, and he usually is, he might even tell you about his famous cousin.

"That's his claim to fame," says wife Jan, in referring to Johnny Depp the actor.

Sorry to disagree. I think the awesome fudge is his claim to fame.

SHOPPERS INFO ?

Address:
128 South Front Avenue
Hours:
8 a.m. – 5 p.m., Monday – Friday
10 a.m. – 3 p.m., Saturday
Closed Sunday
Phone:
606/886-8957
Area Attractions:
Scenic, Jenny Wiley State Park

EASTERN

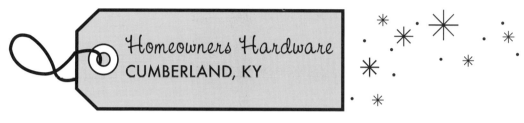

Homeowners Hardware
CUMBERLAND, KY

This is a store you've got to see to believe. In fact, a sign above the front door reads: "You won't believe it."

Homeowners Hardware in Cumberland, Kentucky, is without question one of the most unusual stores in this book. It's difficult to describe for sure. That's why you need to go there.

Jim and Alberta Bullock have owned the store for some 53 years. Customers know when the store is open by the clutter piled outside. Racks of brooms, shovels, tarps, filters, gas cans, pop, and sometimes stuff that hasn't sold in years.

Gwen Blair says it appears to be a marketing tool, but it is a necessity due to the fact that there's no room inside the store for the goods and customers, too.

The cash register sits at the front of the store, and so does the telephone.

"It rings non-stop," says Gwen, "And as luck would have it, most of the time it's always for someone else."

At the front of the store is also a large mural painted across one wall. No one is for sure how long it's been there, but they do agree a long time. The mural depicts a man running from a woman with the caption, "Where Ma Saves Pa's Jack." The regulars don't seem to notice it anymore, but with new folks it draws a chuckle.

"A local artist did the mural sometime back," Gwen says. "He was in need of funds."

Several small

family businesses are also run from the cluttered area around the cash register: rental property, construction, security, mail drop to UPS, and even advice. Oh, did I forget politics? There's plenty of that, too.

At Homeowners Hardware, when they run out of shelf space, it goes on the floor. A trip down one of the cluttered aisles can be an adventure. It seems the only person who knows where a certain item might be is Jim, the owner.

"It may take me awhile, but it's here," he says.

Homeowners Hardware can sometime get very busy, especially when supply trucks arrive. A nearby construction company's employees will pitch-in to help unload, and customers will often answer the phone.

Gwen points out that nearby pop machines sell the second largest amount in town. That should tell you something.

"My dad is 79, he could retire," she says. "But he says this is the only way he gets to see his family."

Yes, this is a store worth seeing!

SHOPPERS INFO ?

Address:
209 Beal Street
Hours:
8 a.m. – 5 p.m., Monday – Saturday
Closed Sunday
Phone:
606/589-4014
Area Attractions:
Kingdom Come State Park, Coal Mine Museum at Benham

EASTERN

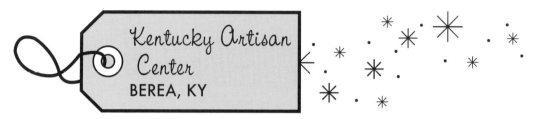

Kentucky Artisan Center
BEREA, KY

I have a friend who rates a business by how clean its restrooms are. His theory is that if the restrooms are clean, it is a well-run business. Works for me.

Not only did one travel publication rate the restrooms at the Kentucky Artisan the cleanest on I-75, but also the best designed.

This is one great place to shop and browse. It's easy to see why well over 600,000 people have shopped here since it opened in 2003.

It all starts with the exterior. The Center is a work of art in itself. The walls, both inside and out, were hand-built by a group of Kentucky stone masons using native limestone quarried near Harrodsburg, Kentucky. Combined with the interior's rich cherry wood, it all makes for a stunning

backdrop for exhibits and displays by more than 650 Kentucky artisans.

It is a common sight for visitors to see rotating exhibits of artisans weaving baskets, stringing brooms, hammering tin, or notching out delicate carvings. Kentucky authors often do book signings here as well.

Jewelry, furniture, quilts, hand-blown glass, soaps and many other Kentucky-made crafts are displayed and sold here.

The Artisan Center is so impressively laid out that it takes on the feel of a museum.

What helps in making this stop even more special is the staff's knowledge about the artisans and their works. They also assist visitors to other area shops, galleries and studios.

The Artisan Center also serves up some very good food, "Kentucky dishes," in its sit-down café. How about a hot brown, bourbon bread pudding, fried chicken or Kentucky-made Valentine's gourmet ice cream.

Great shopping, good food and clean restrooms. Can it get any better than that?

SHOPPERS INFO ?

Address:
I-75, exit 77
Walnut Meadow Road
Hours:
8 a.m. – 8 p.m., daily
Phone:
859/985-5448
Area Attractions:
Berea College, crafts

EASTERN

Log House Craft Gallery
BEREA, KY

as one might expect, the Log House Craft Gallery in Berea is located in a huge log-like structure in the heart of downtown. It's within easy walking distance of just about anything in the area.

Actually, the Log House is a part of Berea College and has been since 1917 when it was built. Initially constructed to house Fireside Weaving, it lays claim to being the oldest and largest craft gallery in Kentucky.

All of the merchandise are literally works of art, handcrafted either by Berea students, local, state and regional artist.

Not only do students make a lot of the crafts, but they work in the gallery as well. During the school year as many as 15 are employed here.

Upon entering the beautiful shop, visitors will see fine handcrafted, traditional furniture, as well as other wood crafts, weavings, ceramics, forged iron items and sturdy one-of-a-kind handmade brooms. All of this is a result of the college's Student Crafts Industries program.

Berea is a small town in Madison County, just off I-75 that is ab-

solutely chocked full of unique shops, and if you're lucky enough to get a room at Boone Tavern for an evening or two, it makes for a great getaway.

The College was founded in 1855, and all of its 1,500 students are required to work a certain number of hours each week to pay for full-tuition scholarships.

The Log House, by being a part of Berea College, puts all its profits back in order to help with these student scholarships.

SHOPPERS INFO ?

Address:
200 Estill Street
Hours:
8 a.m. – 7 p.m., Monday – Saturday
1 p.m. – 5 p.m., Sunday
Call for January hours
Phone:
859/985-3226
Area Attractions:
Berea College, Kentucky Artisan Center, numerous artists and craftsmen

EASTERN

Mickey's
PIKEVILLE, KY

Mickey's Classic Clothing, for several years has offered "big city" shopping for women's fashions without having to leave town.

If you haven't been to Pikeville lately you might not recognize it. After all, this is the town that moved a river and railroad. The 14 years it took to re-route the flood-prone Big Sandy River, has been labeled as "saving-the-town." A note of interest is that it was the second largest earth removal project in the world, second only to the Panama Canal.

Add to that, a state-of-the art Eastern Kentucky Expo Center, sparkling new downtown hotel, a fantastic Medical Center, and a progressive college, and you have a town on the move.

I say all of this about Pikeville, because it sets the stage for Mickey's upscale shop right smack in the middle of downtown.

"In the beginning I was told I could not be exclusive with some of my brands and styles," says owner Mickey England. "But now I pride myself

in being just that. If I see my merchandise in another store, I drop it."

Mickey's likes to say they sell traditional clothing. "It's traditional with a twist," Mickey adds.

A few of those traditional lines are David Brooks, Windridge, Ann Trinity, Dizzy Lizzy, Tyler Boe, Nic and Zoe, and fdj French Dressing. Some select shoes and bath and body products are also featured.

"Our clientele consists of ages 25 to 90," Mickey said. "And we have customers from West Virginia, Virginia, Tennessee, and of course, all over Kentucky. But the true success of our shop is the loyalty of the locals."

Mickey's has been a successful business for 17 years, but when she decided to first move the business downtown she was struggling with a name for her shop.

"I very cleverly came up with cute names, even thinking about naming it after my mother or my daughters," she laughed. "But one of my friends said no matter what you call it, everyone will say "I'm going to Mickey's."

SHOPPERS INFO ?

Address:
223 Second Street
Hours:
10 a.m. – 5 p.m., Monday – Friday
10 a.m. – 3 p.m., Saturday
Closed Sunday
Phone:
606/432-5373
Area Attractions:
Pikeville Cut-Through, Big Sandy Heritage Museum, Hatfield-McCoy Festival

EASTERN

Red Dog & Company
LONDON, KY

ike Angel and his wife Fredi several years ago bought some property in Laurel County where someday they wanted to live. Not only do they live there now, but they also work there!

A log house with a sizeable woodworkers shop nearby is where they spend most of their time handcrafting some of the finest furniture in all of Kentucky.

It's Mike's Mule-Ear chairs and rockers that serve as his signature product, so-called because of the way the back posts of the chairs flair up and out similar to the ears of a mule.

Named for a special pet, the business has evolved to where it involves various family members and friends taking on responsibilities in order to turn out the finished product.

Mike, a former Kentucky State Trooper and special agent for the Bureau of Alcohol, Tobacco and Firearms, began making chairs in 1994, and today he turns out settees, benches, and all sizes of stools and tables.

The 3,600 square foot workshop and showroom, is a whirlwind of activity, and although Angel respects and appreciates the vintage tools

and techniques used by his grandfather, he uses a combination of old and new.

"I use green wood that takes advantage of the natural movement of wood as it dries out," he says. "This ensures the joints remain tight."

He uses a steam generator, from a sauna of all things, to bend the back posts and slats to the desired shape. Chairs are all pegged, no nails here. But he does use glue as an extra precaution.

Kentucky oak, ash, hickory, cherry and walnut are the woods used for most of the chair frames. On occasion Osage orange and wormy chestnut, or burled mesquite are the choice. The woven bottoms are made from flat reed, sea grass cord, Shaker tape or hickory bark.

There aren't chairs like this anywhere else. When you settle into one of these, it's not just the back that fits, or the seat, but your arms, and even your fingers feel good resting on the chairs arms.

A phone call is recommended before you visit.

SHOPPERS INFO ?

Address:
998 Angel Acres
Hours:
9 a.m. – 4:30 p.m., 7 days a week – Call for an appointment
Phone:
606/878-8555
Area Attractions:
Chicken Festival, Levi Jackson State Park

EASTERN

At first blush this shop has been misnamed. Sweet Kreations doesn't begin to give a hint on what is on the inside of this wonderful little shop that sits just off of the main lobby of the Big South Fork Scenic Railway Depot in Stearns.

"We started out as a little candy shop," laughs owner Barbara Edwards. "And now that we have grown into all of this, the name probably doesn't really go with the business."

Do not despair, however, because there still are enough sweet creations behind the counter to keep the name of the shop propped up rather nicely.

Barbara and her sister, Kathy Lockhart, each invested $100 into a little candy/gift business they operated from their homes. That was in 1997.

"We just kept reinvesting our profits and here we are today," smiles Barbara.

From candy, to gift baskets, to toys, to a year-round Christmas landing, this store is a fun place to visit.

"Our specialty," says Barbara, "is our custom designed gift baskets."

It seems like the store is always busy, especially before and after the Big South Fork Scenic Railway train ride. The convenience of being at the depot allows those riding the train to usually browse before the ride and return to buy when they get back.

Peanut butter-chocolate fudge is the top seller here as far as fudge goes. But also very popular is their rock candies, salt water taffy, pull candy, licorice, candy buttons and jawbreakers.

Being located in a depot, you just knew they sell railroad related gifts and toys. Thomas the Tank Engine is a best seller here.

Sweet Kreations also merchandises America Expedition Wildlife and Nature gifts, Barlow Knives, vintage and retro gifts, Webkinz, Virtual Pets, quilted throws, handbags, sterling silver jewelry and Boyd's Bears.

Don't be misled by the name. See for yourself!

Address:
Big South Fork Scenic Railway Depot
100 Henderson Street
Hours:
10 a.m. – 5 p.m., Tuesday – Friday, 10 a.m. – 5 p.m., Saturday
1 p.m. – 5 p.m., Sunday, Closed Monday
Closed first two weeks of January
Phone:
606/376-4050
Area Attractions:
Big South Fork Scenic Railway, Barthell Coal Camp, Daniel Boone National Forest

EASTERN

Tater Knob Pottery
BEREA, KY

Often a business fails to live up to its catchy name. Such is not the case with Tater Knob Pottery and Farm.

Located in Madison County, some 10 miles from Berea, this one-of-a-kind pottery shop and showroom most certainly lives up to what visitors expect: a shopping experience that will stick to the ribs for a long time.

It starts with beautiful scenery at the foothills of Appalachia and continues up, around and over a narrow, winding gravel road until you are there.

A showroom with large windows allows plenty of light to smother and accent the many pieces of "just-made" pottery stacked on table after table.

Sarah Culbreth and husband Jeff Enge are the resident potters here, and since they decided to move to the "outskirts of Berea" more than a quarter of a century ago, the pair has established themselves as high end producers of fine pottery. Their studio, in the same building as the showroom, turns out bowls, vases, cups, mugs, bells, lamps, lanterns, pitchers, glasses, and on and on. All uniquely produced while using experienced

hands to manipulate a glob of clay as it rapidly spins on a flat wheel in front of them. It doesn't take long to realize that this is tedious work.

Both Sarah and Jeff are graduates of Berea College, and took quite a risk when they decided to move away from the town and purchase 30 acres of land.

"In the beginning it was a struggle until we got the word out," offers Jeff. "But now we are growing. It has worked for us."

Tater Knob doesn't wholesale its crafts. "We use a mailing list and count on the folks that come here," says Sarah. "I think our hospitality and the full experience a person has when they visit our showroom and working studio has helped a lot."

Address:
260 Wolf Gap Road – From Berea, State 21 East to U.S. 421, left, 1 mile, turn right on State 594, 3 ½ miles turn left on Wolf Gap Road, ½ mile to Tater Knob

Hours:
9 a.m. – 5 p.m., Monday – Saturday, all year except Christmas and major holidays
Closed Sunday

Phone:
859/986-2167

Area Attractions:
Berea, Snug Hollow B & B

The Black Barn
LOMANSVILLE, KY

Steve and Marla Carter like to keep things simple. That's why they decided to name their business in Lomansville, nine miles north of Paintsville, The Black Barn. After all, they had an old black barn Marla's dad had built, and everyone in the area already knew where it was just by the color of it.

"My late father-in-law, Phillip Clark, cut the timber and built the barn," said Steve. "And the name came about because of the color of the barn."

The color is a story in itself.

A painter came by and told Mr. Clark he would paint the barn and it would never peel or fade. Being a trusting man, he told the painter to go ahead and paint it. To everyone's surprise after more than 30 years it is still black and never peeled.

Those, indeed, were the good old days, and that's exactly the type of store The Black Barn is. It has the feel of a place our grandparents shopped in: hoop cheeses; bulk beans, 16 varieties, displayed and sold out of whiskey barrels; bushel baskets and barrels full of candy. Maybe you've heard of your grandmother or even your great-grandmother talk about

buying "penny candy" when she was a little girl. Well, penny candy is sold here! Kids can fill a special bag in the store and pay only a penny for each piece.

The Black Barn's shelves are full of lots of goodies you'd like for yourself or as a thoughtful gift for others.

Jams, jellies, country hams, bacon, ciders and even their infamous "moonshine jelly."

"Travelers who stop in ask if we have any trouble with the revenuers," laughs Steve.

Shoppers will also find RADA Cutlery, Amish country popcorn, milled flour products, dried apples, peaches, and bananas, canned pickles, Vidalia products, honey and a great selection of produce and garden seed.

SHOPPERS INFO ?

Address:
Kentucky Route 3224 Wiley Branch Road
Hours:
8 a.m. - 8 p.m., Monday - Saturday
8 a.m. - 4 p.m., Wednesday
10 a.m. - 6 p.m., Sunday
Phone:
606/297-2600
Area Attractions:
Country Music Highway, Mountain Home Place, Jenny Wiley State Park

EASTERN

The Frame Up Gallery
ASHLAND, KY

*B*ack in 1977 it was with a loan and a prayer that Bob and Jo Etta Lynch opened up a framing shop in the basement of a large three-floor building in downtown Ashland.

Now, more than 30 years later, that vision continues to define this marvelous shop which now occupies all three floors of the building that also includes Café Zeal that was opened in 1995.

Bob and Jo Etta take pride in what they have created, not only for themselves and their customers, but also consider their business an asset to the community.

"We have been able to provide unparalleled service and quality to our loyal clients," says Jo Etta.

Both Lynches are actively involved in the business, from helping customers with materials, colors, and style to Bob's actually building the frames and cutting the mats.

"His framing perfection is an investment that will last a lifetime," she adds.

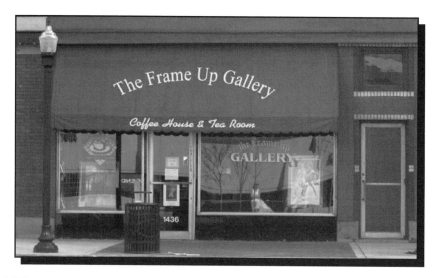

The Gallery stays involved in the latest in home décor that becomes evident by the store's local and regional popularity. It is the norm for the Lynches to bring unique styles and artistic trends back to Ashland from their buying treks to New York, Atlanta and Paris.

"If you don't have a picture to frame or a gift to buy, come to the Gallery to experience Café Zeal," Jo Etta adds. "Our lunches are a creative experience in itself."

The Gallery and the Café have the latest in internet capabilities and a large-screen projector that can be used for business presentations or artist demonstrations. The business also supports local artist and musicians by offering a place for them to exhibit their work and to play their music.

Address:
1436 Winchester Avenue
Hours:
12 noon – 5 p.m., Monday
10 a.m. – 5 p.m., Tuesday – Friday
10 a.m. – 3 p.m., Saturday
Café Hours: 11 a.m. – 3 p.m., Tuesday – Friday
Phone:
606/324-8565
Area Attractions:
Carter Cave State Park

EASTERN

People have all kinds of reasons for opening a business. But George and Tama Ramey, who own and operate The Rusty Hinge in Stambaugh, Kentucky, may have the most no-nonsense reason of all.

"We ran out of room in our house from all of the stuff we had bought and had to do something with it," laughed George. "So we opened a store to put it in."

That was back in 2002, and today this little out-of-the-way store in Johnson County, about eight miles from Paintsville, is going strong.

"George and I had a fondness for collecting just about anything," says Tama. "When we traveled we found ourselves stopping at flea markets, garage sales and roadside sales. We went to the out-of-the-way places to buy things. Our business just happened."

The 14 x 25 foot building with the little front porch almost dares you to peek inside. Stuff is everywhere!

They have several pieces of primitive furniture to include a Hoosier cabinet and handmade rocker. Dolls made in the area are big sellers, as are the soy candles made in Kentucky. "We can hardly keep these in stock. They sell so quickly," Tama offers.

The store also stocks lots of delicious jellies, jams, honey, and sorghum, Kentucky-made bath products that include goat milk and honey soaps. Beautiful hand sewn stitcheries, and books by local authors are also offered.

The Rusty Hinge also sells something

none of the other stores and shops in this book sell.

Outhouses!

"A lot of people are using them for garden sheds," George says with a chuckle.

George, a retired school teacher, points out that as out-of-the-way their store is, they have had customers from 14 states and three foreign countries.

"We're located about a country mile off the Country Music Highway 23," adds George. "We've been told we are pleasant to view, spiritual and peaceful, warm and inviting."

EASTERN

About the Author

Gary P. West grew up in Elizabethtown, Kentucky and attended Western Kentucky University before graduating from the University of Kentucky with a degree in journalism in 1967.

At UK he was a daily sports editor for the *Kentucky Kernel*.

Later he served as editor for the nation's largest civilian enterprise military newspaper at Fort Bragg, North Carolina. From there he went to work as an advertising copywriter in the corporate office of one of the country's largest insurance companies, State Farm Insurance in Bloomington, Illinois.

In 1972 he returned to Kentucky where he began publishing an advertising shopper in Bowling Green.

Along the way, for twelve years, he worked in the athletic department as executive director of the Hilltopper Athletic Foundation at Western Kentucky University, and provided color commentary on the Hilltopper Basketball Network.

In 1993 he became executive director of the Bowling Green Area Convention and Visitors Bureau, where he solidified his background in hospitality. He is a freelance writer for several magazines in addition to writing a syndicated newspaper column, *Out & About... Kentucky Style*, for a number of papers across the state.

In 2005 he wrote the highly acclaimed biography, *King Kelly Coleman—Kentucky's Greatest Basketball Legend*, in 2006, the best selling travel guide *Eating Your Way Across Kentucky*, and in 2007, its sequel *Eating Your Way Across Kentucky—The Recipes*.

Index

Product Index

Other Kentucky bestsellers by Gary P. West & Acclaim Press...

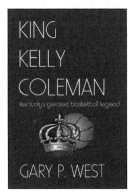

A Basketball Fan's Must Read

In a state where the love of basketball itself is legendary, there are its rare heroes who also, through the dispassionate lens of history, rise to legendary status. When that legend rises so far above the others to acquire mythical or rather, folk hero, proportions - and then enigmatically vanishes- you have King Kelly Coleman.

This shy, humble mountain boy blessed with extraordinary talent and drive captured Kentucky's hearts and its all-time record books with performances that have yet to be equaled - even half a century later. Never before in print, the authorized King Kelly Coleman story, as told by award-winning author Gary P. West, from actual interviews and information from Coleman himself.
Book: 6"x9" hardcover w/dustjacket, 224 pages
ISBN: 0-9773198-0-6
Price: $21.95

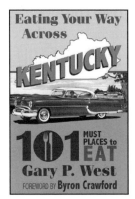

A Traveler's Guide to Local Favorites

There are literally thousands of eating-places in Kentucky. Some are outstanding, some good, some fair and some not so good. One would think it would be easy to identify "101 must places to eat" in the state, but it is a much more daunting task than one would think. What Gary West has done in these pages is to select eateries that in all probability you may not know even about. Oh sure, the locals eat there and know they are great but some of the restaurants are not well known to outsiders – until now.

The criteria for making the 101 are that it cannot be a chain restaurant, and, except for a rare exception, must have been in operation for at least five years. And, of course, the food must be exceptionally delicious.
Book: 6"x9" hardcover, 224 pages
ISBN: 0-9790025-1-6
Price: $19.95

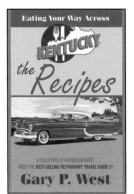

The Recipes that Made them Famous

And now, with *Eating Your Way Across Kentucky: The Recipes*, there is no excuse for not serving these tasty meals at home. With this book you get their recipes.

For the most part this is not about gourmet food, although some recipes might be considered that. If you are expecting recipes that are all about simple food, this is your book!

Cooking in Kentucky is all about simple food! These recipes have been created years ago, usually handed down within families from generation to generation.
Book: 6"x9" hardcover, 224 pages
ISBN: 0-9798802-3-0
Price: $24.95

To order, contact Acclaim Press:
Phone: 1-877-4-AP-BOOK
Online: www.acclaimpress.com

Acclaim Press
— Your Next Great Book —